Astounding Stories of Super-Science

January 1931

Various

Alpha Editions

This edition published in 2024

ISBN : 9789367245323

Design and Setting By
Alpha Editions
www.alphaedis.com
Email - info@alphaedis.com

As per information held with us this book is in Public Domain.
This book is a reproduction of an important historical work. Alpha Editions uses the best technology to reproduce historical work in the same manner it was first published to preserve its original nature. Any marks or number seen are left intentionally to preserve its true form.

"Behold one of those who live in the darkness."

THE DARK SIDE OF ANTRI

By Sewell Peaslee Wright

> Commander John Hanson relates an interplanetary adventure illustrating the splendid Service spirit of the men of the Special Patrol.

AN officer of the Special Patrol Service dropped in to see me the other day. He was a young fellow, very sure of himself, and very kindly towards an old man.

He was doing a monograph, he said, for his own amusement, upon the early forms of our present offensive and defensive weapons. Could I tell him about the first Deuber spheres and the earlier disintegrator rays and the crude atomic bombs we tried back when I first entered the Service?

I could, of course. And I did. But a man's memory does not improve in the course of a century of Earth years. Our scientists have not been able to keep a man's brain as fresh as his body, despite all their vaunted progress. There is a lot these deep thinkers, in their great laboratories, don't know. The whole universe gives them the credit for what's been done, yet the men of action who carried out the ideas—but I'm getting away from my pert young officer.

He listened to me with interest and toleration. Now and then he helped me out, when my memory failed me on some little detail. He seemed to have a very fair theoretical knowledge of the subject.

"It seems impossible," he commented, when we had gone over the ground he had outlined, "that the Service could have done its work with such crude and undeveloped weapons, does it not?" He smiled in a superior sort of way, as though to imply we had probably done the best we could, under the circumstances.

I SUPPOSE I should not have permitted his attitude to irritate me, but I am an old man, and my life has not been an easy one.

"Youngster," I said—like many old people, I prefer spoken conversation—"back in those days the Service was handicapped in every way. We lacked weapons, we lacked instruments, we lacked popular support, and backing. But we had men, in those days, who did their work with the tools that were at hand. And we did it well."

"Yes, sir!" the youngster said hastily—after all, a retired commander in the Special Patrol Service does rate a certain amount of respect, even from these perky youngsters—"I know that, sir. It was the efforts of men like yourself who gave us the proud traditions we have to-day."

"Well, that's hardly true," I corrected him. "I'm not quite so old as that. We had a fine set of traditions when I entered the Service, son. But we did our share to carry them on, I'll grant you that."

"'Nothing Less than Complete Success,'" quoted the lad almost reverently, giving the ancient motto of our service. "That is a fine tradition for a body of men to aspire to, sir."

"True. True." The ring in the boy's voice brought memories flocking. It was a proud motto; as old as I am, the words bring a thrill even now, a thrill comparable only with that which comes from seeing old Earth swell up out of the darkness of space after days of outer emptiness. Old Earth, with her wispy white clouds and her broad seas— Oh, I know I'm provincial, but that is another thing that must be forgiven an old man.

"I imagine, sir," said the young officer, "that you could tell many a strange story of the Service, and the sacrifices men have made to keep that motto the proud boast it is to-day."

"Yes," I told him. "I could do that. I have done so. That is my occupation, now that I have been retired from active service. I—"

"You are a historian?" he broke in eagerly.

I FORGAVE him the interruption. I can still remember my own rather impetuous youth.

"Do I look like a historian?" I think I smiled as I asked him the question, and held out my hands to him. Big brown hands they are, hardened with work, stained and drawn from old acid burns, and the bite of blue electric fire. In my day we worked with crude tools indeed; tools that left their mark upon the workman.

"No. But—"

I waved the explanation aside.

"Historians deal with facts, with accomplishments, with dates and places and the names of great men. I write—what little I do write—of men and high adventures, so that in this time of softness and easy living some few who may read my scribblings may live with me those days when the worlds of the universe were strange to each other, and there were many new things to be found and marveled at."

"And I'll venture, sir, that you find much enjoyment in the work," commented the youngster with a degree of perception with which I had not credited him.

"True. As I write, forgotten faces peer at me through the mists of the years, and strong, friendly voices call to me from out of the past...."

"It must be wonderful to live the old adventures through again," said the young officer hastily. Youth is always afraid of sentiment in old people. Why this should be, I do not know. But it is so.

The lad—I wish I had made a note of his name; I predict a future for him in the Service—left me alone, then, with the thoughts he had stirred up in my mind.

OLD faces ... old voices. Old scenes, too.

Strange worlds, strange peoples. A hundred, a thousand different tongues. Men that came only to my knee, and men that towered ten feet above my head. Creatures—possessed of all the attributes of men except physical form—that belonged only in the nightmare realms of sleep.

An old man's most treasured possessions: his memories. A face drew close out of the flocking recollections; the face of a man I had known and loved more than a brother so many years—dear God, how many years—ago.

Anderson Croy. Search all the voluminous records of the bearded historians, and you will not find his name. No great figure of history was this friend of mine; just an obscure officer on an obscure ship of the Special Patrol Service.

And yet there is a people who owe to him their very existence.

I wonder if they have forgotten him? It would not surprise me.

The memory of the universe is not a reliable thing.

ANDERSON CROY was, like most of the officer personnel of the Special Patrol Service, a native of Earth.

They had tried to make a stoop-shouldered dabbler in formulas out of him, but he was not the stuff from which good scientists are moulded. He was young, when I first knew him, and strong; he had mild blue eyes and a quick smile. And he had a fine, steely courage that a man could love.

I was in command, then, of the *Ertak*, my second ship. I inherited Anderson Croy with the ship, and I liked him from the first time I laid eyes upon him.

As I recall it, we worked together on the *Ertak* for nearly two years, Earth time. We went through some tight places together. I remember our experience, shortly after I took over the *Ertak*, on the monstrous planet Callor, whose tiny, gentle people were attacked by strange, vapid Things that come down upon them from the fastness of the polar cap, and—

But I wander from the story I wish to tell here. An old man's mind is a weak and weary thing that totters and weaves from side to side; like a worn-out ship, it is hard to keep on a straight course.

We were out on one of those long, monotonous patrols, skirting the outer boundaries of the known universe, that were, at that time, before the building of all the many stations we have to-day a dreaded part of the Special Patrol Service routine.

Not once had we landed to stretch our legs. Slowing up to atmospheric speed took time, and we were on a schedule that allowed for no waste of even minutes. We approached the various worlds only close enough to report, and to receive an assurance that all was well. A dog's life, but part of the game.

MY log showed nearly a hundred "All's well" reports, as I remember it, when we slid up to Antri, which was, so far as size is concerned, one of our smallest ports o' call.

Antri, I might add, for the benefit of those who have forgotten their maps of the universe, is a satellite of A-411, which, in turn, is one of the largest bodies of the universe, and both uninhabited and uninhabitable. Antri is somewhat larger than the moon, Earth's satellite, and considerably farther from its controlling body.

"Report our presence, Mr. Croy," I ordered wearily. "And please ask Mr. Correy to keep a sharp watch on the attraction meter." These huge bodies such as A-411 are not pleasant companions at space speeds. A few minute's trouble—space ships gave trouble, in those days—and you melted like a drop of solder when you struck the atmospheric belt.

"Yes, sir!" There never was a crisper young officer than Croy.

I bent over my tables, working out our position and charting our course for the next period. In a few seconds Croy was back, his blue eyes gleaming.

"Sir, an emergency is reported on Antri. We are to make all possible speed, to Oreo, their governing city. I gather that it is very important."

"Very well, Mr. Croy." I can't say the news was unwelcome. Monotony kills young men. "Have the disintegrator ray generators inspected and tested. Turn out the watch below in such time that we may have all hands on duty when we arrive. If there is an emergency, we shall be prepared for it. I shall be with Mr. Correy in the navigating room; if there are any further communications, relay them to me there."

I HURRIED up to the navigating room, and gave Correy his orders.

"Do not reduce speed until it is absolutely necessary," I concluded. "We have an emergency call from Antri, and minutes may be important. How long do you make it to Oreo?"

"About an hour to the atmosphere; say an hour more to set down in the city. I believe that's about right, sir."

I nodded, frowning at the twin charts, with their softly glowing lights, and turned to the television disc, picking up Antri without difficulty.

Of course, back in those days we had the huge and cumbersome discs, their faces shielded by a hood, that would be suitable only for museum pieces now. But they did their work very well, and I searched Antri carefully, at varying ranges, for any sign of disturbances. I found none.

The dark portion, of course, I could not penetrate. Antri has one portion of its face that is turned forever from its sun, and one half that is bathed in perpetual light. The long twilight zone was uninhabited, for the people of Antri are a sun-loving race, and their cities and villages appeared only in the bright areas of perpetual sunlight.

Just as we reduced to atmospheric speed, Croy sent up a message

"The Governing Council sends word that we are to set down on the platform atop the Hall of Government, the large, square white building in the center of the city. They say we will have no difficulty in locating it."

I thanked him and ordered him to stand by for further messages, if any, and picked up the far-flung city of Oreo in my television disc.

THERE was no mistaking the building Croy had mentioned. It stood out from the city around it, cool and white, its mighty columns glistening like crystal in the sun. I could even make out the landing platform, slightly elevated above the roof on spidery arches of silvery metal.

We sped straight for the city at just a fraction of space speed, but the hand of the surface temperature gauge crept slowly toward the red line that marked the dangerous incandescent point. I saw that Correy, like the good navigating officer he was, was watching the gauge as closely as myself, and hence said nothing. We both knew that the Antrians would not have sent a call for help to a ship of the Special Patrol Service if there had not been a real emergency.

Correy had made a good guess in saying that it would take about an hour, after entering the gaseous envelope of Antri, to reach our destination. It was just a few minutes—Earth time, of course—less than that when we settled gently onto the landing platform.

A group of six or seven Antrians, dignified old men, wearing the short, loosely belted white robes that we found were their universal costume, were waiting for us at the exit of the *Ertak*, whose sleek, smooth sides were glowing dull red.

"You have hastened, and that is well, sirs," said the spokesman of the committee. "You find Antri in dire need." He spoke in the universal language, and spoke it softly and perfectly. "But you will pardon me for greeting you with that which is, of necessity, uppermost in my mind, and in the minds of these, my companions.

"Permit me to welcome you to Antri, and to introduce those who extend those greetings." Rapidly, he ran through a list of names, and each of the men bowed gravely in acknowledgment of our greetings. I have never observed a more courteous nor a more courtly people than the Antrians; their manners are as beautiful as their faces.

Last of all, their spokesman introduced himself. Bori Tulber, he was called, and he had the honor of being master of the Council—the chief executive of Antri.

WHEN the introductions had been completed, the committee led our little party to a small, cylindrical elevator which dropped us, swiftly and silently, on a cushion of air, to the street level of the great building. Across a wide, gleaming corridor our conductors led us, and stood aside before a massive portal through which ten men might have walked abreast.

We found ourselves in a great chamber with a vaulted ceiling of bright, gleaming metal. At the far end of the room was an elevated rostrum, flanked on either side by huge, intricate masses of statuary, of some creamy, translucent stone that glowed as with some inner light. Semicircular rows of seats, each with its carved desk, surmounted by numerous electrical controls, occupied all the floor space. None of the seats was occupied.

"We have excused the Council from our preliminary deliberations," explained Bori Tulber, "because such a large body is unwieldy. My companions and myself represent the executive heads of the various departments of the Council, and we are empowered to act." He led us through the great council chamber, and into an anteroom, beautifully decorated, and furnished with exceedingly comfortable chairs.

"Be seated, sirs," the Master of the Council suggested. We obeyed silently, and Bori Tulber stood before, gazing thoughtfully into space.

"I DO not know just where to begin," he said slowly. "You men in uniform know, I presume, but little of this world of ours. I presume I had best begin far back.

"Since you are navigators of space, undoubtedly, you are acquainted with the fact that Antri is a world divided into two parts; one of perpetual night, and the other of perpetual day, due to the fact that Antri revolves but once upon its axis during the course of its circuit of its sun, thus presenting always the same face to our luminary.

"We have no day and night, such as obtain on other spheres. There are no set hours for working nor for sleeping nor for pleasure. The measure of a man's work is the measure of his ambition, or his strength, or his desire. It is so also with his sleep and with his pleasures. It is—it has been—a very pleasant arrangement.

"Ours is a fertile country, and our people live very long and very happily with little effort. We have believed that ours was the nearest of all the worlds to the ideal; that nothing could disturb the peace and happiness of our people. We were mistaken.

"THERE is a dark side to Antri. A side upon which the sun never has shone. A dismal place of gloom, which is like the night upon other worlds.

"No Antrian has, to our knowledge, ever penetrated this part of Antri, and lived to tell of his experience. We do not even till the land close to the twilight zone. Why should we, when we have so much fine land upon which the sun shines bright and fair always, save for the two brief seasons of rain?

"We have never given thought to what might be on the dark face of Antri. Darkness and night are things unknown to us; we know of them only from the knowledge which has come to us from other worlds. And now—now we have been brought face to face with a terrible danger which comes to us from that other side of this sphere.

"A people have grown there. A terrible people that I shall not try to describe to you. They threaten us with slavery, with extinction. Four ara ago (the Antrians have their own system of reckoning time, just as we have on Earth, instead of using the universal system, based upon the enaro. An ara corresponds to about fifty hours, Earth time.) we did not know that such a people existed. Now their shadow is upon all our beautifully sunny country, and unless you can aid us, before other help can reach us, I am convinced that Antri is doomed!"

FOR a moment not one of us spoke. We sat there, staring at the old man who had just ceased speaking.

Only a man ripened and seasoned with the passing of years could have stood there before us and uttered, so quietly and solemnly, words such as had just come from his lips. Only in his eyes could we catch a glimpse of the torment which gripped his soul.

"Sir," I said, and have never felt younger than at that moment, when I tried to frame some assurance to this splendid old man who had turned to me and my youthful crew for succor, "we shall do what it lies within our power to do. But tell us more of this danger which threatens.

"I am no man of science, and yet I cannot see how men could live in a land never reached by the sun. There would be no heat, no vegetation. Is that not so?"

"Would that it were!" replied the Master of the Council, bitterly. "What you say would be indeed the truth, were it not for the great river and seas of our sunny Antri, which bear their heated waters to this dark portion of our world, and make it habitable.

"And as for this danger, there is little to be said. At some time, men of our country, men who fish, or venture upon the water in commerce, have been borne, all unwillingly, across the shadowy twilight zone and into the land of darkness. They did not come back, but they were found there and despoiled of their menores.

"Somehow, these creatures who dwell in darkness determined the use of the menore, and now that they have resolved that they shall rule all this sphere, they have been able to make their threat clear to us. Perhaps"—and Bori Tulber smiled faintly and terribly—"you would like to have that message direct from its bearer?"

"IS that possible, sir?" I asked eagerly, glancing around the room. "How—"

"Come with me," said the Master of the Council gently. "Alone—for too many near him excites this terrible messenger. You have your menore?"

"No. I had not thought there would be need of it." The menores of those days, it should be remembered, were heavy, cumbersome circlets that were worn upon the head like a sort of crown, and one did not go so equipped unless in real need of the device. To-day, of course, your menores are but jeweled trinkets that convey thought a score of times more effectively, and weigh but a tenth as much.

"It is a lack easily remedied." Bori Tulber excused himself with a little bow and hurried out into the great council chamber, to appear again in a moment with a menore in either hand.

"Now, if your companions and mine will excuse us for a moment…." He smiled around the seated group apologetically. There was a murmur of assent, and the old man opened a door in the other side of the room.

"It is not far," he said. "I will go first, and show you the way."

HE led me quickly down a long, narrow corridor to a pair of steep stairs that circled far down into the very foundation of the building. The walls of the corridor and the stairs were without windows, but were as bright as noonday from the ethon tubes which were set into both ceiling and walls.

Silently we circled our way down the spiral stairs, and silently the Master of the Council paused before a door at the bottom—a door of dull red metal.

"This is the keeping place of those who come before the Council charged with wrong doing," explained Bori Tulber. His fingers rested upon and pressed certain of a ring of small white buttons in the face of the door, and it opened swiftly and noiselessly. We entered, and the door closed behind us with a soft thud.

"Behold one of those who live in the darkness," said the Master of the Council grimly. "Do not put on the menore until you have a grip upon yourself: I would not have him know how greatly he disturbs us."

I nodded, dumbly, holding the heavy menore dangling in my hand.

I have said that I have beheld strange worlds and strange people in my life, and it is true that I have. I have seen the headless people of that red world Iralo, the ant people, the dragon-fly people, the terrible carnivorous trees of L-472, and the pointed heads of a people who live upon a world which may not be named. But I have still to see a more terrible creature than that which lay before me now.

HE—or it—was reclining upon the floor, for the reason that he could not have stood. No room save one with a vaulted ceiling such as the great council chamber, could offer room enough for this creature to walk erect.

He was, roughly, a shade better than twice my height, yet I believe he would have weighed but little more. You have seen rank weeds that have grown up in the darkness to reach the sun; if you can imagine a man who had done likewise, you can, perhaps, picture that which I saw before me.

His legs at the thigh were no larger than my arm, and his arms were but half the size of my wrist, and jointed twice instead of but once. He wore a careless garment of some dirty yellow, shaggy hide, and his skin, revealed on feet and arms and face, was a terrible, bloodless white; the dead white of a fish's belly. Maggot white. The white of something that had never known the sun.

The head was small and round, with features that were a caricature of man's. His ears were huge, and had the power of movement, for they cocked forward as we entered the room. The nose was not prominently arched, but the nostrils were wide, and very thin, as was his mouth, which was faintly tinged with dusky blue, instead of healthy red. At one time his eyes had been nearly round, and, in proportion, very large. Now they were but shadowy pockets, mercifully covered by shrunken, wrinkled lids that twitched but did not lift.

HE moved as we entered, and from a reclining position, propped up on the double elbows of one spidery arm, he changed to a sitting position that brought his head nearly to the ceiling. He smiled sickeningly, and a queer, sibilant whispering came from the bluish lips.

"That is his way of talking," explained Bori Tulber. "His eyes, you will note, have been gouged out. They cannot stand the light; they prepared their messenger carefully for his work, you'll see."

He placed his menore upon his head, and motioned me to do likewise. The creature searched the floor with one white, leathery hand, and finally located his menore, which he adjusted clumsily.

"You will have to be very attentive," explained my companion. "He expresses himself in terms of pictures only, of course, and his is not a highly developed mind. I shall try to get him to go over the entire story for us again, if I can make him understand. Emanate nothing yourself; he is easily confused."

I nodded silently, my eyes fixed with a sort of fascination upon the creature from the darkness, and waited.

BACK on the *Ertak* again. I called all my officers together for a conference.

"Gentlemen," I said, "we are confronted with a problem of such gravity that I doubt my ability to describe it clearly.

"Briefly, this civilized, beautiful portion of Antri is menaced by a terrible fate. In the dark portion of this unhappy world there live a people who have the lust of conquest in their hearts—and the means at hand with which to wreck this world of perpetual sunlight.

"I have the ultimatum of this people direct from their messenger. They want a terrible tribute in the form of slaves. These slaves would have to live in perpetual darkness, and wait upon the whims of the most monstrous beings these eyes of mine have ever seen. And the number of slaves demanded would—as nearly as I could gather, mean about a third of the entire population. Further tribute in the form of sufficient food to support these slaves is also demanded."

"But, in God's name, sir," burst forth Croy, his eyes blazing, "by what means do they, propose to inforce their infamous demands?"

"By the power of darkness—and a terrible cataclysm. Their wise men—and it would seem that some of them are not unversed in science—have discovered a way to unbalance this world, so that they can cause darkness to creep over this land that has never known it. And as darkness advances, these people of the sun will be utterly helpless before a race that loves darkness, and can see in it like cats. That, gentlemen, is that fate which confronts this world of Antri!"

THERE was a ghastly silence for a moment, and then Croy, always impetuous, spoke up again.

"How do they propose to do this thing sir?", he asked hoarsely.

"With devilish simplicity. They have a great canal dug nearly to the great polar cap of ice. Should they complete it, the hot waters of their seas will be liberated upon this vast ice field, and the warm waters will melt it quickly. If you have not forgotten your lessons, gentlemen, you will remember, since most of you are of Earth, that our scientists tell us our own world turned over in much this same fashion, from natural means, and established for itself new poles. Is that not true?"

Grave, almost frightened nods travelled around the little semicircle of white, thoughtful faces.

"And is there nothing, sir, that we can do?" asked Kincaide, my second officer, in an awed whisper.

"That is the purpose of this conclave: to determine what may be done. We have our bombs and our rays, it is true, but what is the power of this one ship against the people of half a world? And such a people!" I shuddered, despite myself, at the memory of that grinning creature in the cell far below the floor of the council chamber. "This city, and its thousands, we might save, it is true—but not the whole half of this world. And that is the task the Council and its Master have set before us."

"WOULD it be possible to frighten them?" asked Croy. "I gather that they are not an advanced race. Perhaps a show of power—the rays—the atomic pistol—bombs— Call it strategy, sir, or just plain bluff. It seems the only chance."

"You have heard the suggestion, gentlemen," I said. "Has anyone a better?"

"How does Mr. Croy plan to frighten these people of the darkness?" asked Kincaide, who was always practical.

"By going to their country, in this ship, and then letting events take their course," replied Croy promptly. "Details will have to be settled on the spot, as I see it."

"I believe Mr. Croy is right," I decided. "The messenger of these people must be returned to his own kind; the sooner the better. He has given me a mental map of his country; I believe that it will be possible for me to locate the principal city, in which his ruler lives. We will take him there, and then—may God aid us gentlemen."

"Amen," nodded Croy, and the echo of the word ran from lip to lip like the prayer it was. "When do we start?"

I hesitated for just an instant.

"Now," I brought forth crisply. "Immediately. We are gambling with the fate of a world, a fine and happy people. Let us throw the dice quickly, for the strain of waiting will not help us. Is that as you would wish it, gentlemen?"

"It is, sir!" came the grave chorus.

"Very well. Mr. Croy, please report with a detail of ten men, to Bori Tulber, and tell him of our decision. Bring the messenger back with you. The rest of you, gentlemen, to your stations. Make any preparations you may think advisable. Be sure that every available exterior light is in readiness. Let me be notified the moment the messenger is on board and we are ready to take off. Thank you, gentlemen!"

I HASTENED to my quarters and brought the *Ertak's* log down to the minute, explaining in detail the course of action we had decided upon, and the reasons for it. I knew, as did all the *Ertak's* officers who had saluted so crisply, and so coolly gone about the business of carrying out my orders, that we would return from our trip to the dark side of Antri triumphant or—not at all.

Even in these soft days, men still respect the stern, proud motto of our service: "Nothing Less Than Complete Success." The Special Patrol does what it is ordered to do, or no man returns to present excuses. That is a tradition to bring tears of pride to the eyes of even an old man, in whose hands there is strength only for the wielding of a pen. And I was young, in those days.

It was perhaps a quarter of an hour when word came from the navigating room that the messenger was aboard, and we were ready to depart. I closed the log, wondering, I remember, if I would ever make another entry therein, and, if not, whether the words I had just inscribed would ever see the light of day. The love of life is strong in men so young. Then I hurried to the navigating room and took charge.

Bori Tulber had furnished me with large scale maps of the daylight portion of Antri. From the information conveyed to me by the messenger of the people of darkness—the Chisee they called themselves, as nearly as I could get the sound—I rapidly sketched in the map of the other side of Antri, locating their principal city with a small black circle.

Realising that the location of the city we sought was only approximate, we did not bother to work out exact bearings. We set the *Ertak* on her course at a height of only a few thousand feet, and set out at low atmospheric speed, anxiously watching for the dim line of shadow that marked the twilight zone, and the beginning of what promised to be the last mission of the *Ertak* and every man she carried within her smooth, gleaming body.

"TWILIGHT zone in view, sir," reported Croy at length.

"Thank you, Mr. Croy. Have all the exterior lights and searchlights turned on. Speed and course as at present, for the time being."

I picked up the twilight zone without difficulty in the television disc, and at full power examined the terrain.

The rich crops that fairly burst from the earth of the sunlit portion of Antri were not to be observed here. The Antrians made no effort to till this ground, and I doubt that it would have been profitable to do so, even had they wished to come so close to the darkness they hated.

The ground seemed dank, and great dark slugs moved heavily upon its greasy surface. Here and there strange pale growths grew in patches—twisted, spotted growths that seemed somehow unhealthy and poisonous.

I searched the country ahead, pressing further and further into the line of darkness that was swiftly approaching. As the light of the sun faded, our monstrous searchlights cut into the gloom ahead, their great beams slashing the shadows.

In the dark country I had expected to find little if any vegetable growth. Instead, I found that it was a veritable jungle through which even our searchlight rays could not pass.

How tall the growths of this jungle might be, I could not tell, yet I had the feeling that they were tall indeed. They were not trees, these pale, weedy arms that reached towards the dark sky. They were soft and pulpy, and without leaves; just long naked sickly arms that divided and subdivided and ended in little smooth stumps like amputated limbs.

That there was some kind of activity within the shelter of this weird jungle, was evident enough, for I could catch glimpses, now and then of moving things. But what they might be, even the searching eye of the television disc could not determine.

ONE of our searchlight beams, waving through the darkness like the curious antenna of some monstrous insect, came to rest upon a spot far ahead. I followed the beam with the disc, and bent closer, to make sure my eyes did not deceive me.

I was looking at a vast cleared place in the pulpy jungle—a cleared space in the center of which there was a city.

A city built of black, sweating stone, each house exactly like every other house: tall, thin slices of stone, without windows, chimneys or ornamentation of any kind. The only break in the walls was the slit-like door of each house. Instead of being arranged along streets crossing each other at right angles, these houses were built in concentric circles broken only by four narrow streets then ran from the open space in the center of the city to the four points of the compass. Around the entire city was an exceedingly high wall built of and buttressed with the black, sweating stone of which the houses were constructed.

That it was a densely populated city there was ample evidence. People—they were creatures like the messenger; that the Chisee are a people, despite their terrible shape, is hardly debatable—were running up and down the four radial streets, and around the curved connecting streets, in the wildest confusion, their double-elbowed arms flung across their eyes. But even as I watched, the crowd thinned and melted swiftly away, until the streets of the queer, circular city were utterly deserted.

"THE city ahead is not the one we are seeking, sir?" asked Croy, who had evidently been observing the scene through one of the smaller television discs. "I take it that governing city will be farther in the interior."

"According to my rather sketchy information, yes." I replied. "However, keep all the searchlight operators busy, going over very bit of the country within the reach of their beams. You have men on all the auxiliary television discs?"

"Yes, sir."

"Good. Any findings of interest should be reported to me instantly. And—Mr. Croy!"

"Yes, sir?"

"You might order, if you will, that rations be served all men at their posts." Over such country as this, I felt it would be wise to have every man ready for an emergency. It was, perhaps, as well that I issued this order.

It was perhaps half an hour after we had passed the circular city when, far ahead, I could see the pale, unhealthy forest thinning out. A half dozen of our searchlight beams played upon the denuded area, and as I brought the television disc to bear I saw that we were approaching a vast swamp, in which little pools of black water reflected the dazzling light of our searching beams.

Nor was this all. Out of the swamp a thousand strange, winged things were rising: yellowish, bat-like things with forked tails and fierce hooked beaks. And like some obscene miasma from that swamp, they rose and came straight for the *Ertak*!

INSTANTLY I pressed the attention signal that warned every man on the ship.

"All disintegrator rays in action at once!" I barked into the transmitter. "Broad beams, and full energy. Bird-like creatures, dead ahead; do not cease action until ordered!"

I heard the disintegrator ray generators deepen their notes before I finished speaking, and I smiled grimly, turning to Correy.

"Slow down as quickly and as much as possible, Mr. Correy," I ordered. "We have work to do ahead."

He nodded, and gave the order to the operating room; I felt the forward surge that told me my order was being obeyed, and turned my attention again to the television disc.

The ray operators were doing their work well. The search lights showed the air streaked with fine siftings of greasy dust, and these strange winged creatures were disappearing by the scores as the disintegrator rays beat and played upon them.

But they came on gamely, fiercely. Where there had been thousands, there were but hundreds ... scores ... dozens....

There were only five left. Three of them disappeared at once, but the two remaining came on unhesitatingly, their dirty yellow bat-like wings flapping heavily, their naked heads outstretched, and hooked beaks snapping.

One of them disappeared in a little sifting of greasy dust, and the same ray dissolved one wing of the remaining creature. He turned over suddenly, the one good wing flapping wildly, and tumbled towards the waiting swamp that has spawned him. Then, as the ray eagerly followed him, the last of that hellish brood disappeared.

"Circle slowly, Mr. Correy," I ordered. I wanted to make sure there were none of these terrible creatures left. I felt that nothing so terrible should be left alive—even in a world of darkness.

THROUGH the television disc I searched the swamp. As I had half suspected, the filthy ooze held the young of this race of things: grub-like creatures that flipped their heavy bodies about in the slime, alarmed by the light which searched them out.

"All disintegrator rays on the swamp," I ordered. "Sweep it from margin to margin. Let nothing be left alive there."

I had a well trained crew. The disintegrator rays massed themselves into a marching wall of death, and swept up and down the swamp as a plough turns its furrows.

It was easy to trace their passage, for behind them the swamp disappeared, leaving in its stead row after row of broad, dusty paths. When we had finished there was no swamp: there was only a naked area upon which nothing lived, and upon which, for many years, nothing would grow.

"Good work," I commended the disintegrator ray men. "Cease action." And then, to Correy, "Put her on her course again, please."

AN hour went by. We passed several more of the strange, damp circular cities, differing from the first we had seen only in the matter of size. Another hour passed, and I became anxious. If we were on our proper course, and I had understood the Chisee messenger correctly, we should be very close to the governing city. We should—

The waving beam of one of the searchlights came suddenly to rest. Three or four other beams followed it—and then all the others.

"Large city to port, sir!" called Croy excitedly.

"Thank you. I believe it is our destination. Cut all searchlights except the forward beam. Mr. Correy!"

"Yes, sir."

"You can take her over visually now, I believe. The forward searchlight beam will keep our destination in view for you. Set her down cautiously in the center of the city in any suitable place. And—remain at the controls ready for any orders, and have the operating room crew do likewise."

"Yes, sir," said Correy crisply.

With a tenseness I could not control, I bent over the hooded television disc and studied the mighty governing city of the Chisee.

THE governing city of the Chisee was not unlike the others we had seen, save that it was very much larger, and had eight spoke-like streets radiating from its center, instead of four. The protective wall was both thicker and higher.

There was another difference. Instead of a great open space in the center of the city, there was a central, park-like space, in the middle of which was a massive pile, circular in shape, and built, like all the rest of the city, of the black, sweating rock which seemed to be the sole building material of the Chisee.

We set the *Ertak* down close to the big circular building, which we guessed—and correctly—to be the seat of government. I ordered the searchlight ray to be extinguished the moment we landed, and the ethon tubes that illuminated our ship inside to be turned off, so that we might accustom our eyes as much as possible to darkness, finding our way about with small ethon tube flashlights.

With a small guard, I stood at the forward exit of the *Ertak* and watched the huge circular door back out on its mighty threads, and finally swing to one side on its massive gimbals. Croy—the only officer with me—and I both wore our menores, and carried full expeditionary equipment, as did the guard.

The Chisee messenger, grimacing and talking excitedly in his sibilant, whispering voice, crouched on all fours (he could not stand in that small space) and waited, three men of the guard on either side of him. I placed his menore on his head and gave him simple, forceful orders, picturing them for him as best I could:

"Go from this place and find others of your kind. Tell them that we would speak to them with things such as you have upon your head. Run swiftly!"

"I will run," he conveyed to me, "to those great ones who sent me." He pictured them fleetingly. They were creatures like himself, save that they were elaborately dressed in fine skins of several pale colors, and wore upon their arms, between their two elbows, broad circlets of carved metal which I took to be emblems of power or authority, since the chief of them all wore a very broad band. Their faces were much more intelligent than their messenger had led me to expect, and their eyes, very large and round, and not at all human, were the eyes of thoughtful, reasoning creatures.

DOUBLED on all fours, the Chisee crept through the circular exit, and straightened up. As he did so, from out of the darkness a score or more of his fellows rushed up, gathering around him, and blocking the exit with their reedy legs. We could hear than talking excitedly in high-pitched, squeaky whispers. Then, suddenly I received an expression from the Chisee who wore the menore:

"Those who are with me have come from those in power. They say one of you, and one only, is to come with us to our big men who will learn, through a thing such as I wear upon my head, that which you wish to say to them. You are to come quickly; at once."

"I will come," I replied. "Have those with you make way—"

A heavy hand fell upon my shoulder; a voice spoke eagerly in my ear:

"Sir, you must not go!" It was Croy, and his voice shook with feeling. "You are in command of the *Ertak*; she, and those in her need you. Let me go! I insist, sir!"

I turned in the darkness, quickly and angrily.

"Mr. Croy," I said swiftly, "do you realize that you are speaking to your commanding officer?"

I FELT his grip tighten on my arm as the reproof struck home.

"Yes, sir," he said doggedly. "I do. But I repeat that your duty commands you to remain here."

"The duty of a commander in this Service leads him to the place of greatest danger, Mr. Croy," I informed him.

"Then stay with your ship, sir!" he pleaded, craftily. "This may be some trick to get you away, so that they may attack us. Please! Can't you see that I am right, sir?"

I thought swiftly. The earnestness of the youngster had touched me. Beneath the formality and the "sirs" there was a real affection between us.

In the darkness I reached for his hand; I found it and shook it solemnly—a gesture of Earth which is hard to explain. It means many things.

"Go, then, Andy," I said softly. "But do not stay long. An hour at the longest. If you are not back in that length of time, we'll come after you, and whatever else may happen, you can be sure that you will be well avenged. The *Ertak* has not lost her stinger."

"Thank you, John," he replied. "Remember that I shall wear my menore. If I adjust it to full power, and you do likewise, and stand without the shelter of the *Ertak's* metal hull, I shall be able to communicate with you, should there be any danger." He pressed my hand again, and strode through the exit out into the darkness, which was lit only by a few distant stars.

The long, slim legs closed in around him; like a pigmy guarded by the skeletons of giants he was led quickly away.

THE minutes dragged by. There was a nervous tension on the ship, the like of which I have experienced not more than a dozen times in all my years.

No one spoke aloud. Now and again one man would matter uneasily to another; there would be a swift, muttered response, and silence again. We were waiting—waiting.

Ten minutes went by. Twenty. Thirty.

Impatiently I paced up and down before the exit, the guards at their posts, ready to obey any orders instantly.

Forty-five minutes. I walked through the exit; stepped out onto the cold, hard earth.

I could see, behind me, the shadowy bulk of the *Ertak*. Before me, a black, shapeless blot against the star-sprinkled sky, was the great administrative building of the Chisee. And in there, somewhere, was Anderson Croy. I glanced down at the luminous dial of my watch. Fifty minutes. In ten minutes more—

"John Hanson!" My name reached me, faintly but clearly, through the medium of my menore. "This is Croy. Do you understand me?"

"Yes," I replied instantly. "Are you safe?"

"I am safe. All is well. Very well. Will you promise me now to receive what I am about to send, without interruption?"

"Yes," I replied, thoughtlessly and eagerly. "What is it?"

"I HAVE had a long conference with the chief or head of the Chisee," explained Croy rapidly. "He is very intelligent, and his people are much further advanced than we thought.

"Through some form of communication, he has learned of the fight with the weird birds; it seems that they are—or were—the most dreaded of all the creatures of this dark world. Apparently we got the whole brood of them, and this chief, whose name, I gather, is Wieschien, or something like that, is naturally much impressed.

"I have given him a demonstration or two with my atomic pistol and the flashlight—these people are fairly stricken by a ray of light directly in the eyes—and we have reached very favorable terms.

"I am to remain here as chief bodyguard and adviser, of which he has need, for all is not peaceful, I gather, in this kingdom of darkness. In return, he is to give up his plans to subjugate the rest of Antri; he has sworn to do this by what is evidently, to him, a very sacred oath, witnessed solemnly by the rest of his council.

"Under the circumstances, I believe he will do what he says; in any case, the great canal will be filled in, and the Antrians will have plenty of time to erect a great series of disintegrator ray stations along the entire twilight zone, using the broad fan rays to form a solid wall against which the Chisee could not advance even did they, at some future date, carry out their plans. The worst possible result then would be that the people in the sunlit portion would have to migrate from certain sections, and perhaps would have day and night, alternately, as do other worlds.

"This is the agreement we have reached; it is the only one that will save this world. Do you approve, sir?"

"No! Return immediately, and we will show the Chisee that they cannot hold an officer of the Special Patrol as a hostage. Make haste!"

"IT'S no go, sir," came the reply instantly. "I threatened them first. I explained what our disintegrator rays would do, and Wieschien laughed at me.

"This city is built upon great subterranean passages that lead to many hidden exits. If we show the least sign of hostility the work will be resumed on the canal, and, before we can locate the spot, and stop the work, the damage will be done.

"This is our only chance, sir, to make this expedition a complete success. Permit me to judge this fact from the evidence I have before me. Whatever sacrifice there is to make, I make gladly. Wieschien asks that you depart at once, and in peace, and I know this is the only course. Good-by, sir; convey my salutations to my other friends upon the old *Ertak*, and elsewhere. And now, lest my last act as an officer of the Special Patrol Service be to refuse to obey the commands of my superior officer, I am removing the menore. Good-by!"

I tried to reach him again, but there was no response.

Gone! He was gone! Swallowed up in darkness and in silence!

DAZED, shaken to the very foundation of my being, I stood there between the shadowy bulk of the *Ertak* and the towering mass of the great silent pile that was the seat of government in this strange land of darkness, and gazed up at the dark sky above me. I am not ashamed, now, to say that hot tears trickled down my cheeks, nor that as I turned back to the *Ertak*, my throat was so gripped by emotion that I could not speak.

I ordered the exit closed with a wave of my hand; in the navigating room I said but four words: "We depart at once."

At the third meal of the day I gathered my officers about me and told them, as quickly and as gently as I could, of the sacrifice one of their number had made.

It was Kincaide who, when I had finished, rose slowly and made reply.

"Sir," he said quietly, "We had a friend. Some day, he might have died. Now he will live forever in the records of the Service, in the memory of a world, and in the hearts of those who had the honor to serve with him. Could he—or we—wish more?"

Amid a strange silence he sat down again, and there was not an eye among us that was dry.

I HOPE that the snappy young officer who visited me the other day reads this little account of bygone times.

Perhaps it will make clear to him how we worked, in those nearly forgotten days, with the tools we had at hand. They were not the perfect tools of to-day, but what they lacked, we somehow made up.

That fine old motto of the Service, "Nothing Less Than Complete Success," we passed on unsullied to those who came after us.

I hope these youngsters of to-day may do as well.

IN THE NEXT ISSUE

THE TENTACLES FROM BELOW

A Complete Novelette of An American Submarine's Dramatic Raid on Marauding "Machine-Fish" of the Ocean Floor

By Anthony Gilmore

PHALANXES OF ATLANS

Beginning a Thrilling Two-Part Novel of a Strange Hidden Civilisation

By F. V. W. Mason

THE BLACK LAMP

Another of Dr. Bird's Amazing Exploits

By Captain S. P. Meek

THE PIRATE PLANET

The Conclusion of the Splendid Current Novel

By Charles W. Diffin

AND OTHERS!

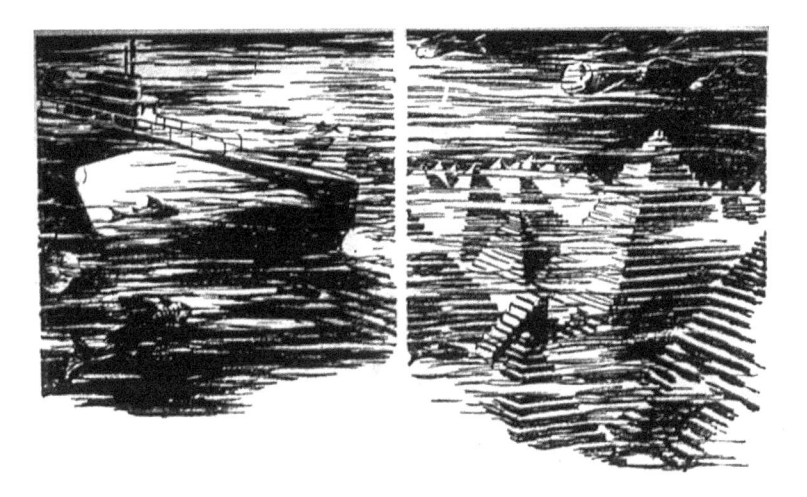

They tilted her rudders and dove to the abysm below.

THE SUNKEN EMPIRE

By H. Thompson Rich

Concerning the strange adventures of Professor Stevens with the Antillians on the floors of the mysterious Sargasso Sea.

"THEN you really expect to find the lost continent of Atlantis, Professor?"

Martin Stevens lifted his bearded face sternly to the reporter who was interviewing him in his study aboard the torpedo-submarine *Nereid*, a craft of his own invention, as she lay moored at her Brooklyn wharf, on an afternoon in October.

"My dear young man," he said, "I am not even going to look for it."

The aspiring journalist—Larry Hunter by name—was properly abashed.

"But I thought," he insisted nevertheless, "that you said you were going to explore the ocean floor under the Sargasso Sea?"

"And so I did." Professor Stevens admitted, a smile moving that gray beard now and his blue eyes twinkling merrily. "But the Sargasso, an area almost equal to Europe, covers other land as well—land of far more recent submergence than Atlantis, which foundered in 9564 B. C., according to Plato. What I am going to look for is this newer lost continent, or island rather—namely, the great island of Antillia, of which the West Indies remain above water to-day."

"Antillia?" queried Larry Hunter, wonderingly. "I never heard of it."

Again the professor regarded his interviewer sternly.

"There are many things you have never heard of, young man," he told him. "Antillia may be termed the missing link between Atlantis and America. It was there that Atlantean culture survived after the appalling catastrophe that wiped out the Atlantean homeland, with its seventy million inhabitants, and it was in the colonies the Antillians established in Mexico and Peru, that their own culture in turn survived, after Antillia too had sunk."

"My Lord! You don't mean to say the Mayas and Incas originated on that island of Antillia?"

"No, I mean to say they originated on the continent of Atlantis, and that Antillia was the stepping stone to the New World, where they built the strange pyramids we find smothered in the jungle—even as thousands of years before the Atlanteans established colonies in Egypt and founded the earliest dynasties of pyramid-building Pharaohs."

LARRY was pushing his pencil furiously.

"Whew!" he gasped. "Some story, Professor!"

"To the general public, perhaps," was the reply. "But to scholars of antiquity, these postulates are pretty well known and pretty well accepted. It remains but to get concrete evidence, in order to prove them to the world at large—and that is the object of my expedition."

More hurried scribbling, then:

"But, say—why don't you go direct to Atlantis and get the real dope?"

"Because that continent foundered so long ago that it is doubtful if any evidence would have withstood the ravages of time," Professor Stevens explained, "whereas Antillia went down no earlier than 200 B. C., archaeologists agree."

"That answers my question," declared Larry, his admiration for this doughty graybeard rising momentarily. "And now, Professor, I wonder if you'd be willing to say a few words about this craft of yours?"

"Cheerfully, if you think it would interest anyone. What would you care to have me say?"

"Well, in the first place, what does the name *Nereid* mean?"

"Sea-nymph. The derivation is from the Latin and Greek, meaning daughter of the sea-god Nereus. Appropriate, don't you think?"

"Swell. And why do you call it a torpedo-submarine? How does it differ from the common or navy variety?"

PROFESSOR STEVENS smiled. It was like asking what was the difference between the sun and the moon, when about the only point of resemblance they had was that they were both round. Nevertheless, he enumerated some of the major modifications he had developed.

Among them, perhaps the most radical, was its motive power, which was produced by what he called a vacuo-turbine—a device that sucked in the water at the snout of the craft and expelled it at the tail, at the time purifying a certain amount for drinking purposes and extracting sufficient oxygen to maintain a healthful atmosphere while running submerged.

Then, the structure of the *Nereid* was unique, he explained, permitting it to attain depths where the pressure would crush an ordinary submarine, while mechanical eyes on the television principle afforded a view in all directions, and locks enabling them to leave the craft at will and explore the sea-bottom were provided.

This latter feat they would accomplish in special suits, designed on the same pneumatic principle as the torpedo itself and capable of sustaining sufficient inflation to resist whatever pressures might be encountered, as well as being equipped with vibratory sending and receiving apparatus, for maintaining communication with those left aboard.

ALL these things and more Professor Stevens outlined, as Larry's pencil flew, admitting that he had spent the past ten years and the best part of his private fortune in developing his plans.

"But you'll get it all back, won't you? Aren't there all sorts of Spanish galleons and pirate barques laden with gold supposed to be down there?"

"Undoubtedly," was the calm reply. "But I am not on a treasure hunt, young man. If I find one single sign of former life, I shall be amply rewarded."

Whereupon the young reporter regarded the subject of his interview with fresh admiration, not unmingled with wonder. In his own hectic world, people had no such scorn of gold. Gee, he'd sure like to go along! The professor could have his old statues or whatever he was looking for. As for himself, he'd fill up his pockets with Spanish doubloons and pieces of eight!

Larry was snapped out of his trance by a light knock on the door, which opened to admit a radiant girl in creamy knickers and green cardigan.

"May I come in, daddy?" she inquired, hesitating, as she saw he was not alone.

"You seem to be in already, my dear," the professor told her, rising from his desk and stepping forward.

Then, turning to Larry, who had also risen, he said:

"Mr. Hunter, this is my daughter, Diane, who is also my secretary."

"I am pleased to meet you, Miss Stevens," said Larry, taking her hand.

And he meant it—for almost anyone would have been pleased to meet Diane, with her tawny gold hair, warm olive cheeks and eyes bluer even than her father's and just as twinkling, just as intelligent.

"She will accompany the expedition and take stenographic notes of everything we observe," added her father, to Larry's amazement.

"What?" he declared. "You mean to say that—that—"

"Of course he means to say that I'm going, if that's what you mean to say, Mr. Hunter," Diane assured him. "Can you think of any good reason why I shouldn't go, when girls are flying around the world and everything else?"

Even had Larry been able to think of any good reason, he wouldn't have mentioned it. But as a matter of fact, he had shifted quite abruptly to an entirely different line of thought. Diane, he was thinking—Diana, goddess of the chase, the huntress! And himself, Larry Hunter—the hunter and the huntress!

Gee, but he'd like to go! What an adventure, hunting around together on the bottom of the ocean!

WHAT a wild dream, rather, he concluded when his senses returned. For after all, he was only a reporter, fated to write about other people's adventures, not to participate in them. So he put away his pad and pencil and prepared to leave.

But at the door he paused.

"Oh, yes—one more question. When are you planning to leave, Professor?"

At that, Martin Stevens and his daughter exchanged a swift glance. Then, with a smile, Diane said:

"I see no reason why we shouldn't tell him, daddy."

"But we didn't tell the reporters from the other papers, my dear," protested her father.

"Then suppose we give Mr. Hunter the exclusive story," she said, transferring her smile to Larry now. "It will be what you call a—a scoop. Isn't that it?"

"That's it."

She caught her father's acquiescing nod. "Then here's your scoop, Mr. Hunter. We leave to-night."

To-night! This was indeed a scoop! If he hurried, he could catch the late afternoon editions with it.

"I—I certainly thank you, Miss Stevens!" he exclaimed. "That'll make the front page!"

As he grasped the door-knob, he added, turning to her father:

"And I want to thank you too, Professor—and wish you good luck!"

Then, with a hasty handshake, and a last smile of gratitude for Diane, he flung open the door and departed, unconscious that two young blue eyes followed his broad shoulders wistfully till they disappeared from view.

BUT Larry was unaware that he had made a favorable impression on Diane. He felt it was the reverse. As he headed toward the subway, that vivid blond goddess of the chase was uppermost in his thoughts.

Soon she'd be off in the *Nereid*, bound for the mysterious regions under the Sargasso Sea, while in a few moments he'd be in the subway, bound under the prosaic East River for New York.

No—damned if he would!

Suddenly, with a wild inspiration, the young reporter altered his course, dove into the nearest phone booth and got his city editor on the wire.

Scoop? This was just the first installment. He'd get a scoop that would fill a book!

And his city editor tacitly O. K.'d the idea.

With the result that when the *Nereid* drew away from her wharf that night, on the start of her unparalleled voyage, Larry Hunter was a stowaway.

THE place where he had succeeded in secreting himself was a small storeroom far aft, on one of the lower decks. There he huddled in the darkness, while the slow hours wore away, hearing only the low hum of the craft's vacuo-turbine and the flux of water running through her.

From the way she rolled and pitched, he judged she was still proceeding along on the surface.

Having eaten before he came aboard, he felt no hunger, but the close air and the dark quarters brought drowsiness. He slept.

When he awoke it was still dark, of course, but a glance at his luminous wristwatch told him it was morning now. And the fact that the rolling and pitching had ceased made him believe they were now running submerged.

The urge for breakfast asserting itself, Larry drew a bar of chocolate from his pocket and munched on it. But this was scanty fare for a healthy young six-footer, accustomed to a liberal portion of ham and eggs. Furthermore, the lack of coffee made him realize that he was getting decidedly thirsty. The air, moreover, was getting pretty bad.

"All in all, this hole wasn't exactly intended for a bedroom!" he reflected with a wry smile.

Taking a chance, he opened the door a crack and sat there impatiently, while the interminable minutes ticked off.

The *Nereid's* turbine was humming now with a high, vibrant note that indicated they must be knocking off the knots at a lively clip. He wondered how far out they were, and how far down.

Lord, there'd be a riot when he showed up! He wanted to wait till they were far enough on their way so it would be too much trouble to turn around and put him ashore.

But by noon his powers of endurance were exhausted. Flinging open the door, he stepped out into the corridor, followed it to a companionway and mounted the ladder to the deck above.

There he was assailed by a familiar and welcome odor—food!

Trailing it to its origin, he came to a pair of swinging doors at the end of a cork-paved passage. Beyond, he saw on peering through, was the mess-room, and there at the table, among a number of uniformed officers, sat Professor Stevens and Diane.

A last moment Larry stood there, looking in on them. Then, drawing a deep breath, he pushed wide the swinging doors and entered with a cheery:

"Good morning, folks! Hope I'm not too late for lunch!"

VARYING degrees of surprise greeted this dramatic appearance. The officers stared, Diane gasped, her father leaped to has feet with a cry.

"That reporter! Why—why, what are you doing here, young man?"

"Just representing the press."

Larry tried to make it sound nonchalant but he was finding it difficult to bear up under this barrage of disapproving eyes—particularly two very young, very blue ones.

"So that is the way you reward us for giving you an exclusive story, is it?" Professor Stevens' voice was scathing. "A representative of the press! A stowaway, rather—and as such you will be treated!"

He turned to one of his officers.

"Report to Captain Petersen that we have a stowaway aboard and order him to put about at once."

He turned to another.

"See that Mr. Hunter is taken below and locked up. When we reach New York, he will be handed over to the police."

"But daddy!" protested Diane, as they rose to comply, her eyes softening now. "We shouldn't be too severe with Mr. Hunter. After all, he is probably doing only what his paper ordered him to."

GRATEFULLY Larry turned toward his defender. But he couldn't let that pass.

"No, I'm acting only on my own initiative," he said. "No one told me to come."

For he couldn't get his city editor involved, and after all it was his own idea.

"You see!" declared Professor Stevens. "He admits it is his own doing. It is clear he has exceeded his authority, therefore, and deserves no sympathy."

"But can't you let me stay, now that I'm here?" urged Larry. "I know something about boats. I'll serve as a member of the crew—anything."

"Impossible. We have a full complement. You would be more of a hindrance than a help. Besides, I do not care to have the possible results of this expedition blared before the public."

"I'll write nothing you do not approve."

"I have no time to edit your writings, young man. My own, will occupy me sufficiently. So it is useless. You are only wasting your breath—and mine."

He motioned for his officers to carry out his orders.

But before they could move to do so, in strode a lean, middle-aged Norwegian Larry sensed must be Captain Petersen himself, and on his weathered face was an expression of such gravity that it was obvious to everyone something serious had happened.

IGNORING Larry, after one brief look of inquiry that was answered by Professor Stevens, he reported swiftly what he had to say.

While cruising full speed at forty fathoms, with kite-aerial out, their wireless operator had received a radio warning to turn back. Answering on its call-length, he had demanded to know the sender and the reason for the message, but the information had been declined, the warning merely being repeated.

"Was it a land station or a ship at sea?" asked the professor.

"Evidently the latter," was the reply. "By our radio range-finder, we determined the position at approximately latitude 27, longitude 65."

"But that, Captain, is in the very area we are headed for."

"And that, Professor, makes it all the more singular."

"But—well, well! This is indeed peculiar! And I had been on the point of turning back with our impetuous young stowaway. What would you suggest, sir?"

Captain Petersen meditated, while Larry held his breath.

"To turn back," he said at length, in his clear, precise English, "would in my opinion be to give the laugh to someone whose sense of humor is already too well developed."

"Exactly!" agreed Professor Stevens, as Larry relaxed in relief. "Whoever this practical joker is, we will show him he is wasting his talents—even though it means carrying a supernumerary for the rest of the voyage."

"Well spoken!" said the captain. "But as far as that is concerned, I think I can keep Mr. Hunter occupied."

"Then take him, and welcome!"

Whereupon, still elated but now somewhat uneasy, Larry accompanied Captain Petersen from the mess-room; started to, that is. But at a glance of sympathy from Diane, he dared call out:

"Say—hold on, folks! I haven't had lunch yet!"

WHEN young Larry Hunter reported to the captain of the *Nereid*, after this necessary meal, he found that the craft had returned to the surface.

Assigned a pair of powerful binoculars, he was ordered to stand watch in the conning-tower and survey the horizon in every direction, in an effort to sight the vessel that had sent out that mysterious radio, but though he cast his good brown eyes diligently through those strong lenses, he saw not so much as a smoke tuft upon the broad, gray-blue surface of the hazy Atlantic.

Gradually, however, as the afternoon wore away, something else came in view. Masses of brownish seaweed, supported by small, berry-like bladders, began drifting by. Far apart at first, they began getting more and more dense, till at last, with a thrill, he realized that they were drawing into that strange area known as the Sargasso Sea.

Shortly after this realization dawned, he was ordered below, and as the tropic sun was sinking over that eery floating tombstone, which according to Professor Stevens marked a nation's grave, the *Nereid* submerged.

Down she slid, a hundred fathoms or more, on a long, even glide that took her deep under that veiling brown blanket.

IN the navigating room now, Larry stood with the captain, the professor and Diane, studying an illuminated panel on which appeared a cross of five squares, like a box opened out.

The central square reproduced the scene below, while those to left and right depicted it from port and starboard, and those to front and rear revealed the forward and aft aspects of the panorama, thus affording a clear view in every direction.

This, then, was the television device Professor Stevens had referred to the previous afternoon, its mechanical eyes enabling then to search every square inch of those mysterious depths, as they cruised along.

It was the central square that occupied their attention chiefly, however, as they stood studying the panel. While the others represented merely an unbroken vista of greenish water, this one showed the sea floor as clearly as though they had been peering down into a shallow lagoon through a glass-bottomed boat, though it must have been a quarter of a mile below their cruising level.

A wonderful and fearsome sight it was to Larry: like something seen in a nightmare—a fantastic desert waste of rocks and dunes, with here and there a yawning chasm whose ominous depths their ray failed to penetrate, and now and then a jutting plateau that would appear on the forward square and cause Captain Petersen to elevate their bow sharply.

But more thrilling than this was their first glimpse of a sunken ship—a Spanish galleon, beyond a doubt!

There she lay, grotesquely on her side, half rotted, half buried in the sand, but still discernible. And to Larry's wildly racing imagination, a flood of gold and jewels seemed to pour from her ruined coffers.

TURNING to Diane, he saw that her eyes too were flashing with intense excitement.

"Say!" he exclaimed. "Why don't we stop and look her over? There may be a fortune down there!"

Professor Stevens promptly vetoed the suggestion, however.

"I must remind you, young man," he said severely, "that this is not a treasure hunt."

Whereupon Larry subsided; outwardly, at least. But when presently the central square revealed another and then another sunken ship, it was all he could do to contain himself.

Now, suddenly, Diane cried out:

"Oh, daddy, look! There's a modern ship! A—a freighter, isn't it?"

"A collier, I would say," was her father's calm reply. "Rather a large one, too. *Cyclops*, possibly. She disappeared some years ago, en route from the Barbados to Norfolk. Or possibly it is any one of a dozen other steel vessels that have vanished from these seas in recent times. The area of the Sargasso, my dear, is known as 'The Port of Missing Ships.'"

"But couldn't we drop down and make sure which ship it is?" she pleaded, voicing the very thought Larry had been struggling to suppress.

At the professor's reply, however, he was glad he had kept quiet.

"We could, of course," was his gentle though firm rebuke, "but if we stopped to solve the mystery of every sunken ship we shall probably see during this cruise, we would have time for nothing else. Nevertheless, my dear, you may take a short memorandum of the location and circumstances, in the present instance."

Whereupon he dictated briefly, while Larry devoted his attention once more to the central square.

SUDDENLY, beyond a dark pit that seemed to reach down into the very bowels of the earth, rose an abrupt plateau—and on one of its nearer elevations, almost directly under then, loomed a monumental four-sided mound.

"Say—hold on!" called Larry. "Look at that, Professor! Isn't that a building of some kind?"

Martin Stevens looked up, glanced skeptically toward the panel. But one glimpse at what that central square revealed, and his skepticism vanished.

"A building?" he cried in triumph. "A building indeed! It is a pyramid, young man!"

"Good Lord!"

"Oh, daddy! Really?"

"Beyond a doubt! And look—there are two other similar structures, only smaller!"

Struggling for calm, he turned to Captain Petersen, who had taken his eyes from the forward square and was peering down as well upon those singular mounds.

"Stop! Descend!" was his exultant command. "This is my proof! We have discovered Antillia!"

SWIFTLY the *Nereid* dropped to that submerged plateau.

In five minutes, her keel was resting evenly on the smooth sand beside the largest of the three pyramids.

Professor Stevens then announced that he would make a preliminary investigation of the site at once.

"For, otherwise, I for one would be quite unable to sleep tonight!" declared the graybeard, with a boyish chuckle.

He added that Diane would accompany him.

At this latter announcement, Larry's heart sank. He had hoped against hope that he might be invited along with them.

But once again his champion came to his aid.

"We really ought to let Mr. Hunter come with us, daddy, don't you think?" she urged, noting his disappointment. "After all, it was he who made the discovery."

"Very true," said her father, "but I had not thought it necessary for anyone to accompany us. In the event anyone does, Captain Petersen should have that honor."

But this honor the captain declined.

"If you don't mind, sir, I'd prefer to stay with the ship," he said, quietly. "I haven't forgotten that radio warning."

"But surely you don't think anyone can molest us down here?" scoffed the professor.

"No, but I'd prefer to stay with the ship just the same, sir, if you don't mind."

"Very well"—with a touch of pique. "Then you may come along if you care to, Mr. Hunter."

If he cared to!

"Thanks, Professor!" he said with a grateful look toward Diane. "I'd be keen to!"

SO he accompanied them below, where they donned their pressure-suits—rubber affairs rather less cumbersome than ordinary deep-sea diving gear, reinforced with steel wire and provided with thick glass goggles and powerful searchlights, in addition to their vibratory communication apparatus and other devices that were explained to Larry.

When he had mastered their operation, which was rendered simple by reason of the fact that they were so nearly automatic, the trio stepped into a lock on the floor of the ship and Professor Stevens ordered them to couple their suits to air-valve connections on the wall, at the same time admitting water by opening another valve.

Swiftly the lock flooded, while their suits inflated.

"All right?" came his vibratory query.

"Right!" they both answered.

"Then stand by for the heavy pressure."

Wider now he opened the water-valve, letting the ocean in, while at the same time their suits continued inflating through their air-valve connections.

To his surprise, Larry found himself no more inconvenienced by the pressure than he had been from the moment the submarine dove to its present depth. Indeed, most of the air that was coming into his suit was filling the reinforced space between its inner and outer layers, much as the *Nereid* held air under pressure between her two thick shells.

"All right now?" called out the professor's vibrator.

"Right!" they called back again.

"Then uncouple your air-valve connections and make ready."

They did so; and he likewise.

Then, advancing to a massive door like that of a vault, he flung back its powerful clamps, dragged it open—and there beyond, its pressure equaled by that within the lock, loomed the black tide of the ocean bottom.

AWED by this solemn sight, tingling with a sense of unparalleled adventure, Larry stood there a moment, peering out over the threshold of that untrodden world.

Then he followed Diane and her father into its beckoning mystery....

Their searchlights cutting bright segments into the dark, they proceeded toward the vast mound that towered ahead, pushing through a weird realm of phosphorescent fish and other marine creatures.

As they neared it, any possible doubt that it was in fact a pyramid vanished. Corroded by the action of salt water and covered with the incrustations of centuries, it nevertheless presented unmistakable evidence of human construction, rising in steps of massive masonry to a summit shadowy in the murk above.

As Larry stood gazing upon that mighty proof that this submerged plateau had once stood forth proudly above the sea, he realized that he was a party to one of the most profound discoveries of the ages. What a furore this would make when he reported it back to his New York paper!

But New York seemed remote indeed, now. Would they ever get back? What if anything went wrong with their pressure-suits—or if they should become lost?

He glanced back uneasily, but there gleamed the reassuring lights of the *Nereid*, not a quarter of a mile away.

Diane and her father were now rounding a corner of the pyramid and he followed them, his momentary twinge of anxiety gone.

FOR some moments, Professor Stevens prowled about without comment, examining the huge basal blocks of the structure and glancing up its sloping sides.

"You see, I was right!" he declared at length. "This is not only a man-made edifice but a true pyramid, embodying the same architectural principles as the Mayan and Egyptian forms. We see before us the visible evidence of a sunken empire—the missing link between Atlantis and America."

No comments greeted this profound announcement and the professor continued:

"This structure appears to be similar in dimensions with that of the pyramid of Xochicalco, in Mexico, which in turn approximates that of the "Sacred Hill" of Atlantis, mentioned by Plato, and which was the prototype of both the Egyptian and Mayan forms. It was here the Antillians, as the Atlanteans had taught them to do, worshipped their grim gods and performed the human sacrifices they thought necessary to appease them. And it was here, too, if I am not mistaken, that—"

Suddenly his vibratory discourse was broken into by a sharp signal from the submarine:

"Pardon interruption! Hurry back! We are attacked!"

At this, the trio stood rigid.

"Captain Petersen! Captain Petersen!" Larry heard the professor call. "Speak up! Give details! What has happened?"

But an ominous silence greeted the query.

Another moment they stood there, thoroughly dismayed now. Then came the professor's swift command:

"Follow me—quickly!"

He was already in motion, retracing his steps as fast as his bulky suit would permit. But as he rounded the corner of the pyramid, they saw him pause, stand staring. And as they drew up, they in turn paused; stood staring, too.

With sinking hearts, they saw that the *Nereid* was gone.

STUNNED by this disaster, they stood facing one another—three lone human beings, on the bottom of the Atlantic ocean, their sole means of salvation gone.

Professor Stevens was the first to speak.

"This is unbelievable!" he said. "I cannot credit it. We must have lost our senses."

"Or our bearings!" added Diane, more hopefully. "Suppose we look around the other side."

As for Larry, a darker suspicion flashed through his mind. Captain Petersen! Had he seized his opportunity and led the crew to mutiny, in the hope of converting the expedition into a treasure hunt? Was that the reason he had been so willing to remain behind?

He kept his suspicion to himself, however, and accompanied Diane and her father on a complete circuit of the pyramid; but, as he feared, there was no sign of the *Nereid* anywhere. The craft had vanished as completely as though the ocean floor had opened and swallowed her up.

But no, not as completely as that! For presently the professor, who had proceeded to the site where they left the craft resting on the sand, called out excitedly:

"Here—come here! There are tracks! Captain Petersen was right! They were attacked!"

Hurrying to the scene, they saw before them the plain evidences of a struggle. The ocean bottom was scuffed and stamped, as though by many feet, and a clear trail showed where the craft had finally been dragged away.

Obviously there was but one thing to do and they did it. After a brief conference, they turned and followed the trail.

IT led off over the plateau a quarter mile or more, in an eastward direction, terminating at length beside one of the smaller pyramids—and there lay the *Nereid*, apparently unharmed.

But her lights were out and there came no answer to their repeated calls, so they judged she must be empty.

What had happened to Captain Petersen and his crew? What strange sub-sea enemy had overcome them? What was now their fate?

Unanswerable question! But one thing was certain. Larry had misjudged the captain in suspecting him of mutiny. He was sorry for this and resolved he would make amends by doing all in his power to rescue him and his men, if they were still living.

Meanwhile his own plight, and that of Diane and her father, was critical. What was to be done?

Suddenly, as all three stood there debating that question, Professor Stevens uttered an exclamation and strode toward the pyramid. Following him with their eyes, they saw him pass through an aperture where a huge block of stone had been displaced—and disappear within.

The next moment they had joined him, to find themselves in a small flooded chamber at whose far end a narrow gallery sloped upward at a sharp angle.

The floor and walls were tiled, they noted, and showed none of the corrosion of the exterior surfaces. Indeed, so immaculate was the room that it might have been occupied but yesterday.

As they stood gazing around in wonder, scarcely daring to draw the natural inferences of this phenomena, there came a rasping sound, and, turning toward the entrance, they saw a massive section of masonry descend snugly into place.

They were trapped!

STANDING there tense, speechless, they waited, wondering what would be the next move of this strange enemy who held them now so surely in his power.

Nor had they long to wait.

Almost immediately, there issued a gurgling sound from the inclined gallery, and turning their eyes in the direction of this new phenomena, they saw that the water level was receding, as though under pressure from above.

"Singular!" muttered Professor Stevens. "A sort of primitive lock. It seems incredible that human creatures could exist down here, but such appears to be the case."

Larry had no desire to dispute the assumption, nor had Diane. They stood there as people might in the imminence of the supernatural, awaiting they knew not what.

Swiftly the water receded.

Now it was scarcely up to their waists, now plashing about their ankles, and now the room was empty.

The next moment, there sounded a rush of feet—and down the gallery came a swarm of the strangest beings any of them had ever seen.

They were short, thin, almost emaciated, with pale, pinched faces and pasty, half-naked bodies. But they shimmered with ornaments of gold and jade, like some strange princes from the realm of Neptune—or rather, like Aztec chieftains of the days of Cortes, thought Larry.

Blinking in the glare of the searchlights, they clamored around their captives, touching their pressure-suits half in awe and chattering among themselves.

THEN one of them, larger and more regally clad than the rest, stepped up and gestured toward the balcony.

"They obviously desire us to accompany them above," said the professor, "and quite as obviously we have little choice in the matter, so I suggest we do so."

"Check!" said Larry.

"And double-check!" added Diane.

So they started up, preceded by a handful of their captors and followed by the main party.

The gallery seemed to be leading toward the center of the pyramid, but after a hundred feet or so it turned and continued up at a right angle, turning twice more before they arrived at length in another stone chamber, smaller than the one below.

Here their guides paused and waited for the main party.

There followed another conference, whereupon their leader stepped up again, indicating this time that they were to remove their suits.

At this, Professor Stevens balked.

"It is suicide!" he declared. "The air to which they are accustomed here is doubtless at many times our own atmospheric pressure."

"But I don't see that there's anything to do about it," said Larry, as their captors danced about them menacingly. "I for one will take a chance!"

And before they could stop him, he had pressed the release-valve, emitting the air from his suit—slowly, at first, then more and more rapidly, as no ill effects seemed to result.

Finally, flinging off the now deflated suit, he stepped before them in his ordinary clothes, calling with a smile:

"Come on out, folks—the air's fine!"

THIS statement was somewhat of an exaggeration, as the air smelt dank and bad. But at least it was breathable, as Diane and her father found when they emerged from their own suits.

They discovered, furthermore, now that their flashlights were no longer operating, that a faint illumination lit the room, issuing from a number of small crystal jars suspended from the walls: some sort of phosphorescence, evidently.

Once again the leader of the curious throng stepped up to them, beaming now and addressing Professor Stevens in some barbaric tongue, and, to their amazement, he replied in words approximating its harsh syllables.

"Why, daddy!" gasped Diane. "How can you talk to him?"

"Simply enough," was the reply. "They speak a language which seems to be about one-third Basque, mixed oddly with Greek. It merely proves another hypothesis of mine, namely, that the Atlantean influence reached eastward to the Pyrenees mountains and the Hellenic peninsula, as well as to Egypt."

WHEREUPON he turned and continued his conversation, haltingly it is true and with many gestures, but understandably nevertheless.

"I have received considerable enlightenment as to the mystery of this strange sunken empire," he reported, turning back to them at length. "It is a singular story this creature tells, of how his country sank slowly beneath the waves, during the course of centuries, and of how his ancestors adapted themselves by degrees to the present conditions. I shall report it to you both, in detail, when time affords. But the main thing now is that a man similar to ourselves has conquered their country and set himself up as emperor. It is to him we are about to be taken."

"But it doesn't seem possible!" exclaimed Diane. "Why, how could he have got down here?"

"In a craft similar to our own, according to this creature. Heaven knows what it is we are about to face! But whatever it is, we will face it bravely."

"Check and double-check!" said Larry, with a glance toward Diane that told her she would not find him wanting.

They were not destined to meet the test just then, however, for just at that moment a courier in breech-clout and sandals dashed up the gallery and burst into the room, bearing in his right hand a thin square of metal.

Bowing, he handed it to the leader of the pigmy throng, with the awed word:

"*Cabiri!*"

At this, Professor Stevens gave a start.

"A message from their high priests!" he whispered.

Whatever it contained, the effect produced on the reader was profound. Facing his companions, he addressed them gravely. Then, turning from the room, he commanded the captives to follow.

THE way led back down the inclined gallery to a point where another door now stood open, then on down until finally the passage leveled out into a long, straight tunnel.

This they traversed for fully a mile, entering at length a large, square chamber where for a moment they paused.

"I judge we are now at the base of the large pyramid," the professor voiced in an undertone. "It would naturally be the abode of the high priests."

"But what do you suppose they want with us?" asked Diane.

"That I am not disposed to conjecture," was her father's reply.

But the note of anxiety in his voice was not lost on Diane, nor on Larry, who pressed her hand reassuringly.

Now their captors led them from the room through a small door opening on another inclined gallery, whose turns they followed until all were out of breath from the climb.

It ended abruptly on a short, level corridor with apertures to left and right.

Into the latter they were led, finding themselves in a grotesquely furnished room, lit dimly by phosphorescent lamps.

Swiftly the leader addressed Professor Stevens. Then all withdrew. The aperture was closed by a sliding block of stone.

FOR a moment they stood there silent, straining their eyes in the gloom to detect the details of their surroundings, which included several curious chairs and a number of mattings strewn on the tiled floor.

"What did he say?" asked Diane at length, in a tremulous voice.

"He said we will remain here for the night," her father replied, "and will be taken before the high priests at dawn."

"At dawn!" exclaimed Larry. "How the deuce do they know when it is dawn, down here?"

"By their calendars, which they have kept accurately," was the answer. "But there are many other questions you must both want to ask, so I shall anticipate them by telling you now what I have been able to learn. Suppose we first sit down, however. I for one am weary."

Whereupon they drew up three of those curious chairs of some heavy wood carved with the hideous figures of this strange people's ancient gods, and Professor Stevens began.

THEIR sunken empire, as he had surmised, had indeed been the great island of Antillia and a colony of Atlantis. A series of earthquakes and tidal waves such as engulfed their homeland ages before had sent it down, and the estimated archaeological date of the final submergence—namely, 200 B. C.—was approximately correct.

But long before this ultimate catastrophe, the bulk of the disheartened population had migrated to Central and South America, founding the Mayan and Incan dynasties. Many of the faithful had stayed on, however, among them most of the Cabiri or high priests, who either were loath to leave their temples or had been ordered by their gods to remain.

At any rate, they had remained, and as the great island sank lower and lower, they had fortified themselves against the disaster in their pyramids, which by then alone remained above the surface.

These, too, had gradually disappeared beneath the angry waters, however, and with them had disappeared the steadfast priests and their faithful followers, sealing their living tombs into air-tight bell-jars that retained the atmosphere.

This they had supplemented at first by drawing it down from above, but as time went by they found other means of getting air; extracting it from the sea water under pressure, by utilizing their subterranean volcanoes, in whose seething cauldrons the gods had placed their salvation; and it was this process that now provided them with the atmosphere which had so amazed their captives.

But naturally, lack of sunshine had produced serious degeneration in their race, and that accounted for their diminutive forms and pale bodies. Still, they had been able to survive with a degree of happiness until some ten or a dozen years ago, when a strange enemy had come down in a great metal fish, like that of these new strangers, and with a handful of men had conquered their country.

This marauder was after their gold and had looted their temples ruthlessly, carrying away its treasures, for which they hated him with a fury that only violation of their most sacred deities could arouse. Long ago they would have destroyed him, but for the fact that he possessed terrible weapons which were impossible to combat. But they were in smouldering rebellion and waited only the support of their gods, when they would fall on this oppressor and hurl him off.

That, though it left many things unexplained, was all the professor had been able to gather from his conversation with the leader of their captors. He ended, admitting regretfully that he was still in ignorance of what fate had befallen Captain Petersen and the crew of the *Nereid.*

"PERHAPS this fellow in the other submarine has got them," suggested Larry.

"But why weren't we taken to him too?" asked Diane. "What do you suppose they want with us, anyway, daddy?"

"That, my dear, as I told you before," replied her father, "I am not disposed to conjecture. Time will reveal it. Meanwhile, we can only wait."

As before, there was a note of anxiety in his voice not lost on either of them. And as for Larry, though he knew but little of those old religions, he knew enough to realize that their altars often ran with the blood of their captives, and he shuddered.

With these grim thoughts between them, the trio fell silent.

A silence that was interrupted presently by the arrival of a native bearing a tray heaped with strange food.

Bowing, he placed it before them and departed.

Upon examination, the meal proved to consist mainly of some curious kind of steamed fish, not unpalatable but rather rank and tough. There were several varieties of fungus, too, more or less resembling mushrooms and doubtless grown in some sunless garden of the pyramid.

These articles, together with a pitcher of good water that had obviously been distilled from the sea, comprised their meal, and though it was far from appetizing, they ate it.

But none of the three slept that night, though Diane dozed off for a few minutes once or twice, for their apprehension of what the dawn might hold made it impossible, to say nothing of the closeness of the air in that windowless subterranean room.

Slowly, wearily, the hours dragged by.

At length the native who had brought their food came again. This time he spoke.

"He says we are now to be taken before the high priests," Professor Stevens translated for them.

Almost with relief, though their faces were grave, they stepped out into the corridor, where an escort waited.

FIVE minutes later, after proceeding along an inclined gallery that wound ever upward, they were ushered into a vast vaulted chamber lit with a thousand phosphorescent lamps and gleaming with idols of gold and silver, jewels flashing from their eyes.

High in the dome hung a great golden disc, representing the sun. At the far end, above a marble altar, coiled a dragon with tusks of ivory and scales of jade, its eyes two lustrous pearls.

And all about the room thronged priests in fantastic head-dress and long white robes, woven through elaborately with threads of yellow and green.

At the appearance of the captives, a murmur like a chant rose in the still air. Someone touched a brand to the altar and there was a flash of flame followed by a thin column of smoke that spiraled slowly upward.

Now one of the priests stepped out—the supreme one among them, to judge from the magnificence of his robe—and addressed the trio, speaking slowly, rhythmically.

As his strange, sonorous discourse continued, Professor Stevens grew visibly perturbed. His beard twitched and he shifted uneasily on his feet.

FINALLY the discourse ceased and the professor replied to it, briefly. Then he turned grave eyes on Larry and Diane.

"What is it?" asked the latter, nervously. "What did the priest say, daddy?"

Her father considered, before replying.

"Naturally, I did not gather everything," was his slow reply, "but I gathered sufficient to understand what is afoot. First, however, let me explain that the dragon you see over there represents their deity Tlaloc, god of the sea. In more happy circumstances, it would be interesting to note that the name is identified with the Mayan god of the same element."

He paused, as though loath to go on, then continued:

"At any rate, the Antillians have worshipped Tlaloc principally, since their sun god failed them. They believe he dragged down their empire in his mighty coils, through anger with them, and will raise it up again if appeased. Therefore they propose today to—"

"Daddy!" cried Diane, shrinking back in horror, while a chill went up Larry's spine. "You mean—mean that—"

"I mean, my poor child, that we are about to be sacrificed to the dragon god of the Antillians."

THE words were no more than uttered, when with a weird chant the Cabiri closed in on their victims and led them with solemn ceremonial toward the altar.

In vain did Professor Stevens protest. Their decision had been made and was irrevocable. Tlaloc must be appeased. Lo, even now he roared for the offering!

They pointed to the dragon, from whose nostrils suddenly issued hissing spurts of flame.

Larry fumed in disgust at the cheap hocus-pocus of it—but the next moment a more violent emotion swept over him as he saw Diane seized and borne swiftly to that loathsome shrine.

But even as he lunged forward, the professor reached his daughter's side. Throwing himself in front of her, he begged them to spare her, to sacrifice him instead.

The answer of the priests was a blow that knocked the graybeard senseless, and lifting Diane up, half-swooning, they flung her upon the altar.

"Mr. Hunter! Larry!" came her despairing cry.

She struggled up and for a moment her blue eyes opened, met his beseechingly.

That was enough—that and that despairing cry, "Larry!"

With the strength of frenzy, he flung off his captors, rushed to her aid, his hard fists flailing.

The pigmies went down in his path like grain before the scythe. Reaching the altar, he seized the priest whose knife was already upraised, and, lifting him bodily, flung him full into the ugly snout of that snorting dragon.

Then, as a wail of dismay rose from the Cabiri, at this supreme sacrilege, he seized the now unconscious Diane and retreated with her toward the door.

BUT there spears barred his escape; and now, recovered from the first shock of this fearful affront to their god, the priests started toward him.

Standing at bay, with that limp, tender burden in his arms, Larry awaited the end.

As the maddened horde drew near, she stirred, lifted her pale face and smiled, her eyes still shut.

"Oh, Larry!"

"Diane!"

"You saved me. I won't forget."

Then, the smile still lingering, she slipped once more into merciful oblivion, and as Larry held her close to his heart, a new warmth kindled there.

But bitterness burned in his heart, too. He had saved her—won her love, perhaps—only to lose her. It wasn't fair! Was there no way out?

The priests were close now, their pasty faces leering with fierce anticipation of their revenge, when suddenly, from down the gallery outside that guarded door, came the sharp crash of an explosion, followed by shouts and the rush of feet.

At the sound, the priests trembled, fled backward into the room and fell moaning before their idols, while the quaking guards strove frantically to close the door.

BUT before they could do so, in burst a half dozen brawny sailors in foreign uniform, bearing in their hands little black bulbs that looked suspiciously like grenades. Shouting in a tongue Larry could not distinguish above the uproar, they advanced upon the retreating guards and priests.

Then, when all were herded in the far corner of the room, the sailors backed toward the door. Motioning for Larry and Diane to clear out, they raised those sinister little missiles, prepared to fling them.

"Wait!" cried Larry, thinking of Professor Stevens.

And releasing Diane, who had revived, he rushed forward, seized the prostrate savant from amid the unresisting Cabiri, and bore him to safety.

"Daddy!" sobbed Diane, swaying to meet them.

"Back!" shouted one of the sailors, shoving them through the door.

The last glimpse Larry had of that fateful room was the horde of priests and guards huddled before their altar, voices lifted in supplication to that hideous dragon god.

Then issued a series of blinding flashes followed by deafening explosions, mingled with shrieks of anguish.

Sickened, he stood there, as the reverberations died away.

PRESENTLY, when it was plain no further menace would come from that blasted temple, their rescuers led the trio back down those winding galleries, and through that long, straight tunnel to the smaller pyramid.

Professor Stevens had recovered consciousness by now and was able to walk, with Larry's aid, though a matted clot of blood above his left ear showed the force of the blow he had received.

The way, after reaching the smaller pyramid, led up those other galleries they had mounted the night before.

This time, undoubtedly, they were to be taken before that mysterious usurping emperor. And what would be the result of that audience? Would it but plunge them from the frying pan into the fire, wondered Larry, or would it mean their salvation?

Anyway, he concluded, no fate could be worse than the hideous one they had just escaped. But if only Diane could be spared further anguish!

He glanced at her fondly, as they walked along, and she returned him a warm smile.

Now the way led into a short, level passage ending in a door guarded by two sailors with rifles. They presented arms, as their comrades came up, and flung open the door.

As he stepped inside, Larry blinked in amazement, for he was greeted by electric lights in ornate clusters, richly carpeted floors, walls hung with modern paintings—and there at the far end, beside a massive desk, stood an imposing personage in foreign naval uniform of high rank, strangely familiar, strangely reminiscent of war days.

Even before the man spoke, in his guttural English, the suspicion those sailors had aroused crystallized itself.

A German! A U-boat commander!

"GREETINGS, gentlemen—and the little lady," boomed their host, with heavy affability. "I see that my men were in time. These swine of Antillians are a tricky lot. I must apologize for them—my subjects."

The last word was pronounced with scathing contempt.

"We return greetings!" said Professor Stevens. "To whom, might I ask, do we owe our lives, and the honor of this interview?"

Larry smiled. The old graybeard was up to his form, all right!

"You are addressing Herr Rolf von Ullrich," the flattered German replied, adding genially: "commander of one of His Imperial Majesty's super-submarines during the late war and at present Emperor of Antillia."

To which the professor replied with dignity that he was greatly honored to make the acquaintance of so exalted a personage, and proceeded in turn to introduce himself and party. But Von Ullrich checked him with a smile.

"The distinguished Professor Stevens and his charming daughter need no introduction, as they are already familiar to me through the American press and radio," he said. "While as for Mr. Hunter, your Captain Petersen has already made me acquainted with his name."

At the mention of the commander of the *Nereid*, all three of them gave a start.

"Then—then my captain and crew are safe?" asked the professor, eagerly.

"Quite," Von Ullrich assured him. "You will be taken to them presently. But first there are one or two little things you would like explained—yes? Then I shall put to you a proposal, which if acceptable will guarantee your safe departure from my adopted country."

Whereupon the German traced briefly the events leading up to the present.

DURING the last months of the war, he had been placed in command of a special U-boat known as the "mystery ship"—designed to resist depth-charges and embodying many other innovations, most of them growing out of his own experience with earlier submarines.

One day, while cruising off the West Indies, in wait for some luckless sugar boat, he had been surprised by a destroyer and forced to submerge so suddenly that his diving gear had jammed and they had gone to the bottom. But the craft had managed to withstand the pressure and they had been able to repair the damage, limping home with a bad leak but otherwise none the worse for the experience.

The leak repaired and the hull further strengthened, he had set out again. But when in mid-Atlantic the Armistice had come, and rather than return to a defeated country, subject possibly to Allied revenge, he had persuaded his crew to remain out and let their craft be reported missing.

What followed then, though Von Ullrich masked it in polite words, was a story of piracy, until they found by degrees that there was more gold on the bottom of the ocean than the top; and from this to the discovery of the sunken empire where he now held reign was but a step.

They had thought at first they were looting only empty temples—but, finding people there, had easily conquered them, though ruling them, he admitted, was another matter. As, for instance, yesterday, when the priests had interfered with his orders and carried his three chief captives off to sacrifice.

"Where now, but for me, you would be food for their gods!" he ended. "And if you do not find my hospitality altogether to your liking, friends, remember that you came uninvited. In fact, if you will recall, you came despite my explicit warning!"

BUT since they were here, he told them, they might be willing to repay his good turn with another.

Whereupon Von Ullrich launched into his proposal, which was that Professor Stevens place the *Nereid* at his disposal for visiting the depths at the foot of the plateau, where lay the capital of the empire, he said—a magnificent metropolis known as the City of the Sun and modeled after the great Atlantean capital, the City of the Golden Gates, and the depository of a treasure, the greedy German believed, that was the ransom of the world.

The professor frowned, and for a moment Larry thought he was going to remind their host that this was not a treasure hunt.

"Why," he asked instead, "do you not use your own submarine for the purpose?"

"Because for one thing, she will not stand the pressure, nor will our suits," was the reply. "And for another, she is already laden with treasure, ready for an—er—forced abdication!" with a sardonic laugh.

"Then have you not enough gold already?"

"For myself, yes. But there are my men, you see—and men who have glimpsed the treasures of the earth are not easily satisfied, Professor. But have no fear. You shall accompany us, and, by your aid, shall pay your own ransom."

VON ULLRICH made no mention of the alternative, in case the aid was refused, but the ominous light Larry caught in his cold gray eyes spoke as clearly as words.

So, since there was nothing else to do, Professor Stevens agreed.

Whereupon the audience terminated and they were led from the presence of this arrogant German to another apartment, where they were to meet Captain Petersen and the crew of the *Nereid*.

As they proceeded toward it, under guard, Larry wondered why Von Ullrich had even troubled to make the request, when he held it in his power to take the craft anyway.

But after the first joyful moment of reunion, it was a mystery no longer, for Captain Petersen reported that immediately upon their capture, the commander of the U-boat had tried to force him to reveal the operation of the *Nereid*, but that he had steadfastly refused, even though threatened with torture.

And to think, it came to Larry with a new twinge of shame, that he had suspected this gallant man of mutiny!

THAT very morning, while Professor Stevens and his party were still exchanging experiences with Captain Petersen and the members of the crew, Von Ullrich sent for them and they gathered with his own men in the small lock-chamber at the base of the pyramid.

There they were provided with temporary suits by their host, since their own—which they brought along—could be inflated only from the *Nereid*.

Beside her, they noted as they emerged in relays, the U-boat was now moored.

Entering their own craft, they got under way at once and headed swiftly westward toward the brink of the plateau. Most of Von Ullrich's crew were with them, though a few had been left behind to guard against any treachery, on the part of the now sullen and aroused populace.

Slipping out over the edge of that precipitous tableland, they tilted her rudders and dove to the abysm below.

Presently the central square of the illuminated panel in the navigating room showed three great concentric circles, enclosed by a quadrangle that must have been miles on a side—and within this vast sunken fortress lay a city of innumerable pyramids and temples and palaces.

The German's eyes flashed greedily as he peered upon this vision.

"There you are!" he exclaimed, quivering with excitement. "Those circles, that square: what would you judge they were, Professor?"

"I would judge that originally they were the canals bearing the municipal water supply," Martin Stevens told him quietly, suppressing his own excitement, "for such was said to be the construction of the City of the Golden Gates; but now I judge they are walls raised on those original foundations by the frantic populace, when the submergence first began, in a vain effort to hold back the tides that engulfed them."

"And do you think they are of gold?"

"Frankly, no; though I have no doubt you will find plenty of that element down there."

Nor was the prediction wrong, for modern eyes had never seen such a treasure house as they beheld when presently the *Nereid* came to rest outside that ancient four-walled city and they forced their way inside.

THOUGH the walls were not of gold, the inner gates were, and the temples were fairly bursting with the precious metal, as well as rare jewels, the eyes of a thousand idols gleaming with rubies and emeralds.

But where was the populace, amid all this prodigious wealth? Was there no life down here?

Von Ullrich declared through the vibrator of his pressure-suit that he had heard there was. And as though in substantiation, many of the temples showed the same bell-jar construction as the pyramids above, though even stouter, revealing evidences of having been occupied very recently; but all were flooded and empty. The city was as a city of the dead.

This ominous sign did not deter the "emperor," however. Ruthlessly he and his men looted those flooded temples, forcing Professor Stevens and his party to lend aid in the orgy of pillage.

And all the time, Larry had an uneasy feeling of gathering furtive hosts about them, waiting—waiting for what?

He confided his fears to no one, though he noted with relief that Von Ullrich seemed to sense these unseen presences too, for he proceeded with caution and always kept a strong guard outside.

BY early afternoon, the *Nereid* was one great coffer-chest.

But still the rapacious U-boat commander was unsatisfied, though Professor Stevens began to have doubts if his craft could lift that massive weight of plunder to the top of the plateau.

"One more load and we go," he soothed. "A few more pretties for the little lady!"

Larry writhed, and should have suspected then and there—but as it was, the blow fell unexpected, stunning.

Filing from the lock, they failed to notice that Von Ullrich and his crew hung back, until there came a sudden, guttural command, whereupon Diane was seized and the massive door flung shut in their faces.

Appalled by this overwhelming disaster, the party stood for a moment motionless, speechless. Then, as one, Larry and the professor rushed forward and beat upon that barred hatch, calling upon Von Ullrich to open it.

From within the submarine, through their vibrators, they heard him laugh.

"*Auf Wiedersehen!*" he toasted them. "I now have all the treasure I want! The rest I leave to you! Help yourselves!"

Even as he spoke, the *Nereid's* auxiliary propellers started churning the water. Slowly, sluggishly, like some great gorged fish, the sturdy craft moved off, lifted her snout, headed upward.

PROFESSOR STEVENS bowed his head, and Larry could well picture the grief that distorted the graybeard's face, inside that owl-eyed helmet.

"Cheer up!" he said, though his own face was twisted with anguish. "Perhaps—"

Then he paused—for how could he say that perhaps the situation wasn't as bad as it seemed, when it was obviously hopeless?

"My poor Diane!" moaned the professor. "Poor child. Poor child!"

As for Captain Petersen and the crew, they said nothing. Perhaps they were thinking of Diane, perhaps of themselves. At least, they knew it was over.

Or so they thought. But to Larry, suddenly, occurred a gleam of hope. That strange sense of unseen presences! It was bizarre, of course, but doesn't a drowning person catch at straws? And Lord knows they were drowning, if ever anyone was!

He turned and confided to Professor Stevens his idea, which was to retrace their steps within the city gates, seek out the populace and throw themselves on their mercy.

The stricken savant, too, grasped at the straw.

"It seems fantastic, but after all it is a chance," he admitted.

So they pushed back into that great submerged city, with Captain Petersen and his skeptical crew. They entered one of the largest of the temples, wandered forlornly through its flooded halls and corridors, seeking some sign of these alleged beings Larry had sensed.

Nor was their search unrewarded, for suddenly the captain himself, most skeptical of all, cried out:

"Listen! Did you hear that?"

There was no need to ask the question, for all had heard. It was a rasping sound, as of some great door swinging shut, followed almost immediately by a rushing gurgle—and as they stood there tense, the water level began rapidly receding.

Even while it was still plashing about their ankles, a secret block of masonry slid back and a horde of Antillians burst in upon them.

WHAT happened then, happened with a rush that left them dazed.

Unable to talk directly with the pigmies, by reason of their pressure-suits, which they dared not remove, they started gesturing with them, trying to explain their predicament and make known that they bore them no ill-will, but the creatures waved for them to cease and led them swiftly through the now waterless temple.

"Well, I guess it's all up!" said Larry, adding with dismal humor: "They're probably going to finish that meal they started feeding their dragon last night!"

No one laughed, nor made any comment, and he relapsed into silence, realizing that they probably held him responsible for this latest disaster.

Leaving the temple, their captors led them into a passage that was level for a time, then inclined sharply. It was laborious going but they struggled on.

"I believe they know we are not their enemies!" declared Professor Stevens, at length, to everyone's cheer. "They seem to be leading us back to the plateau by some underground passage."

"Let's hope so!" said Larry. "Perhaps I had the right hunch after all."

"But my poor Diane!" came the professor's sorrowing after-thought. "That fiend Von Ullrich could never get the *Nereid* up safely."

"I think perhaps he could, with Miss Stevens to help him," put in Captain Petersen, his usual optimism returning. "She is thoroughly familiar with the craft's operation."

"That is so," her father admitted, his tone brighter. "But—"

"Of course it's so!" exclaimed Larry, breaking off any less hopeful reflections. "So cheerio, folks, as the English say. We'll make it yet!"

But in his heart, he was tormented with doubt for Diane's safety....

THE trail was growing eery, now, and precipitous. To their right rose a sheer cliff. To their left, the path fell off abruptly to a gigantic caldron where red flames leaped and waned.

"Looks like something out of Dante's 'Inferno'!" muttered Larry, with a shudder.

"The volcano where they distill their atmosphere, evidently," commented Professor Stevens. "It would have been interesting, in other circumstances, to observe the process."

"Not to me, it wouldn't!"

Larry was glad when they had passed that seething hell-pot and were once more proceeding through a long, dark gallery.

But everywhere, though their guides were but a handful, was a sense of those unseen presences, of gathering, furtive hosts about them, waiting—waiting for what?

What was this strange sense of tension, of foreboding, that hung in the air? Was the professor wrong? Were they being led to their doom, after all?

He was soon to know, for now the gallery they had been traversing levelled out into a series of short passages, each barred by a heavy stone door, and finally they were led into a small, square room, barely large enough to admit them all.

There, with gestures toward the far end, their guides left them.

The door closed, and almost immediately another on the opposite side opened, slowly at first, then wider and wider, admitting a rush of water that promptly filled the room.

Stepping wonderingly out, they found themselves on the upper level, beside the second of the two smaller pyramids.

"WHEW!" gasped Larry, as they stood looking around, still a little dazed. "These people are sure quick-change artists! First they try to feed you to their gods, then they save you from almost as bad a fate. Dizzy, I call it!"

"Quite understandable, I should say," declared the professor. "Unable to cope with Von Ullrich themselves, they think perhaps we may be able to."

"Well, let's hope they're right!" grimly. "If once I get my hands on him—"

He broke off suddenly, as Captain Petersen called out:

"The *Nereid*! There she is!"

Following with their eyes the bright segment cut into the murky depths by his flashlight, they saw the familiar outlines of their craft; and close beside her lay the U-boat.

A feverish activity seemed to be going on between the two submarines.

"They're changing cargo!" cried Larry. "Quick! We've got them now!"

But the progress they were able to make, hampered by their heavy suits, was maddeningly slow. Their searchlights, moreover, betrayed their approach. Before they could reach the scene, most of the sailors had abandoned their task and piled into the U-boat.

Arms swinging wildly, Von Ullrich stood beside it, trying to rally then. Refusing to risk combat, however, since they were unable to use their deadly hand-grenades under water, they continued clambering up the sides of their submersible and shoving down through its conning-tower hatch.

Now a figure in a familiar pressure-suit broke away and started toward the advancing party.

It was Diane!

EVEN as he recognized her, Larry saw Von Ullrich lunge forward, seize his captive and mount to the conning-tower with her—but before the German could thrust her into the hatch, he had reached the U-boat's side and clambered to her rescue.

Dropping Diane, Von Ullrich wheeled to face his assailant. They grappled, fell to the deck, rolled over and over.

But suddenly, as they were struggling, there came a sound that caused the German to burst free and leap to his feet.

It was the sound of engines under them!

Ignoring Larry now, Von Ullrich staggered to the conning-tower hatch. It was battened fast. Frantically he beat on it.

This much Larry saw, as he knelt there getting his breath. Then he rose, took Diane by the arm and led her down. And he was none too soon, for with a lunge the U-boat got under way.

But she seemed unable to lift her loot-laden mass from the ocean floor, and headed off crazily across the plateau, dragging her keel in the sand.

With fascinated horror, they watched the craft's erratic course, as it swung loggily westward and headed toward that yawning abysm from which they had all so lately risen.

The last sight they had of the U-boat was as it reached the brink, its despairing commander still standing in the conning-tower, hammering vainly on that fast-bound hatch; then they turned away faint, as the doomed craft plunged down, stern up, into those crushing depths.

PROFESSOR STEVENS now joined them.

"A lesson in avarice," he said gravely, when he had greeted his daughter with heartfelt relief. "And a typical fate of fortune hunters! Let that be a lesson to you, young man."

"Amen!" said Larry.

"But what happened, my dear?" asked the professor of Diane, a moment later. "Why were they in such a hurry to be off?"

"Because the sensible Antillians seized their opportunity and overcame their guards, while we were below," was her reply. "When we got back, we found the pyramids flooded, so there was nothing else for them to do but go."

So that was the explanation of those gathering, furtive hosts in the lower level, thought Larry. Now he knew what they had been waiting for! They had been waiting for that usurping vandal to depart.

And how they must be gloating now, down there!

"But why were they so eager to abandon the *Nereid*?" asked the savant, still puzzled. "It it a better boat than theirs, even if I do say so myself."

"Because I put it out of commission, directly we got back up here," replied Diane. "But not permanently!" she added, with what Larry knew was a smile, though he couldn't see her face, of course, through the helmet of her pressure-suit.

"Little thoroughbred!" he exclaimed, half to himself.

"What did you say, Mr. Hunter?—Larry, I mean," she inquired.

"N—nothing," he replied uneasily.

"Fibber!" said Diane. "I heard you the first time!"

"Just wait till I get out of this darned suit!" said Larry.

"I guess I can wait that long!" she told him.

And if Professor Stevens heard any of this, it went in one ear and out the other, for he was thinking what a report he would have to make to his confrères when they got home—particularly with half a boatload of assorted idols for proof.

He pressed the tiny switch in the flame-tool's handle just as Arlok came through the door

By Hal K. Wells

A strange man of metal comes to Earth on a dreadful mission.

HE sat in a small half-darkened booth well over in the corner—the man with the strangely glowing blue-green eyes.

The booth was one of a score that circled the walls of the "Maori Hut," a popular night club in the San Fernando Valley some five miles over the hills from Hollywood.

It was nearly midnight. Half a dozen couples danced lazily in the central dancing space. Other couples remained tête-à-tête in the secluded booths.

In the entire room only two men were dining alone. One was the slender gray-haired little man with the weirdly glowing eyes. The other was Blair Gordon, a highly successful young attorney of Los Angeles. Both men had the unmistakable air of waiting for someone.

Blair Gordon's college days were not so far distant that he had yet lost any of the splendid physique that had made him an All-American tackle. In any physical combat with the slight gray-haired stranger, Gordon knew that he should be able to break the other in two with one hand.

Yet, as he studied the stranger from behind the potted palms that screened his own booth. Gordon was amazed to find himself slowly being overcome by an emotion of dread so intense that it verged upon sheer fear. There was something indescribably alien and utterly sinister in that dimly seen figure in the corner booth.

The faint eery light that glowed in the stranger's deep-set eyes was not the lambent flame seen in the chatoyant orbs of some night-prowling jungle beast. Rather was it the blue-green glow of phosphorescent witch-light that flickers and dances in the night mists above steaming tropical swamps.

The stranger's face was as classically perfect in its rugged outline as that of a Roman war-god, yet those perfect features seemed utterly lifeless. In the twenty minutes that he had been intently watching the stranger, Gordon would have sworn that the other's face had not moved by so much as the twitch of an eye-lash.

THEN a new couple entered the Maori Hut, and Gordon promptly forgot all thought of the puzzlingly alien figure in the corner. The new arrivals were a vibrantly beautiful blond girl and a plump, sallow-faced man in the early forties. The girl was Leah Keith, Hollywood's latest screen sensation. The man was Dave Redding, her director.

A waiter seated Leah and her escort in a booth directly across the room from that of Gordon. It was a maneuver for which Gordon had tipped lavishly when he first came to the Hut.

A week ago Leah Keith's engagement to Blair Gordon had been abruptly ended by a trivial little quarrel that two volatile temperaments had fanned into flames which apparently made reconciliation impossible. A miserably lonely week had finally ended in Gordon's present trip to the Maori Hut. He knew that Leah often came there, and he had an overwhelming longing to at least see her again, even though his pride forced him to remain unseen.

Now, as he stared glumly at Leah through the palms that effectively screened his own booth, Gordon heartily regretted that he had ever come. The sight of Leah's clear fresh beauty merely made him realize what a fool he had been to let that ridiculous little quarrel come between them.

Then, with a sudden tingling thrill, Gordon realized that he was not the only one in the room who was interested in Leah and her escort.

Over in the half-darkened corner booth the eery stranger was staring at the girl with an intentness that made his weird eyes glow like miniature pools of shimmering blue-green fire. Again Gordon felt that vague impression of dread, as though he were in the presence of something utterly alien to all human experience.

GORDON turned his gaze back to Leah, then caught his breath sharply in sudden amaze. The necklace about Leah's throat was beginning to glow with the same uncanny blue-green light that shone in the stranger's eyes! Faint, yet unmistakable, the shimmering radiance pulsed from the necklace in an aura of nameless evil.

And with the coming of that aura of weird light at her throat, a strange trance was swiftly sweeping over Leah. She sat there now as rigidly motionless as some exquisite statue of ivory and jet.

Gordon stared at her in stark bewilderment. He knew the history of Leah's necklace. It was merely an oddity, and nothing more—a freak piece of costume jewelry made from fragments of an Arizona meteorite. Leah had worn the necklace a dozen times before, without any trace of the weird phenomena that were now occurring.

Dancers again thronged the floor to the blaring jazz of the negro orchestra while Gordon was still trying to force his whirling brain to a decision. He was certain that Leah was in deadly peril of some kind, yet the nature of that peril was too bizarre for his mind to imagine.

Then the stranger with the glowing eyes took matters into his own hands. He left his booth and began threading his way through the dancers toward Leah. As he watched the progress of that slight gray-haired figure Gordon refused to believe the evidence of his own eyes. The thing was too utterly absurd—yet Gordon was positive that the strong oak floor of the dancing space was visibly swaying and creaking beneath the stranger's mincing tread!

THE stranger paused at Leah's booth only long enough to utter a brief low-voiced command. Then Leah, still in the grip of that strange trance, rose obediently from her seat to accompany him.

Dave Redding rose angrily to intercept her. The stranger seemed to barely brush the irate director with his finger tips, yet Redding reeled back as though struck by a pile-driver. Leah and the stranger started for the door. Redding scrambled to his feet again and hurried after them.

It was then that Gordon finally shook off the stupor of utter bewilderment that had held him. Springing from his booth, he rushed after the trio.

The dancers in his way delayed Gordon momentarily. Leah and the stranger were already gone when he reached the door. The narrow little entrance hallway to the Hut was deserted save for a figure sprawled there on the floor near the outer door.

It was the body of Dave Redding. Gordon shuddered as he glanced briefly down at the huddled figure. A single mighty blow from some unknown weapon had crumpled the director's entire face in, like the shattered shell of a broken egg.

GORDON charged on through the outer door just as a heavy sedan came careening out of the parking lot. He had a flashing glimpse of Leah and the stranger in the front seat of the big car.

Gordon raced for his own machine, a powerful low-slung roadster. A single vicious jab at the starting button, and the big motor leaped into roaring life. Gordon shot out from the parking lot onto the main boulevard. A hundred yards away the sedan was fleeing toward Hollywood.

Gordon tramped hard on the accelerator. His engine snarled with the unleashed fury of a hundred horsepower. The gap between the two cars swiftly lessened.

Then the stranger seemed to become aware for the first time that he was being followed. The next second the big sedan accelerated with the hurtling speed of a flying bullet. Gordon sent his own foot nearly to the floor. The roadster jumped to eighty miles an hour, yet the sedan continued to leave it remorselessly behind.

The two cars started up the northern slope of Cahuenga Pass with the sedan nearly two hundred yards ahead, and gaining all the time. Gordon wondered briefly if they were to flash down the other side of the Pass and on into Hollywood at their present mad speed.

Then at the summit of the Pass the sedan swerved abruptly to the right and fled west along the Mulholland Highway. Gordon's tires screamed as he swerved the roadster in hot pursuit.

THE dark winding mountain highway was nearly deserted at that hour of the night. Save for an occasional automobile that swerved frantically to the side of the road to dodge the roaring onslaught of the racing cars, Gordon and the stranger had the road to themselves.

The stranger seemed no longer to be trying to leave his pursuer hopelessly behind. He allowed Gordon to come within a hundred yards of him. But that was as near as Gordon could get, is spite of the roadster's best efforts.

Half a dozen times Gordon trod savagely upon his accelerator in a desperate attempt to close the gap, but each time the sedan fled with the swift grace of a scudding phantom. Finally Gordon had to content himself with merely keeping his distance behind the glowing red tail-light of the car ahead.

They passed Laurel Canyon, and still the big sedan bored on to the west. Then finally, half a dozen miles beyond Laurel Canyon, the stranger abruptly left the main highway and started up a narrow private road to the crest of one of the lonely hills. Gordon slowly gained in the next two miles. When the road ended in a winding gravelled driveway into the grounds of what was apparently a private estate, the roadster was scarcely a dozen yards behind.

The stranger's features as he stood there stiffly erect in the vivid glare of the roadster's headlights were still as devoid of all expression as ever. The only things that really seemed alive in that masque of a face were the two eyes, glowing eery blue-green fire like twin entities of alien evil.

Gordon wasted no time in verbal sparring. He motioned briefly to Leah Keith's rigid form in the front seat of the sedan.

"Miss Keith is returning to Hollywood with me," he said curtly. "Will you let her go peaceably, or shall I—?" He left the question unfinished, but its threat was obvious.

"Or shall you do what?" asked the stranger quietly. There was an oddly metallic ring in his low even tones. His words were so precisely clipped that they suggested some origin more mechanical than human.

"Or shall I take Miss Keith with me by force?" Gordon flared angrily.

"You can try to take the lady by force—if you wish." There was an unmistakable jeering note in the metallic tones.

The taunt was the last thing needed to unleash Gordon's volatile temper. He stepped forward and swung a hard left hook for that expressionless masque of a face. But the blow never landed. The stranger dodged with uncanny swiftness. His answering gesture seemed merely the gentlest possible push with an outstretched hand, yet Gordon was sent reeling backward a full dozen steps by the terrific force of that apparently gentle blow.

RECOVERING himself, Gordon grimly returned to the attack. The stranger again flung out one hand in the contemptuous gesture with which one would brush away a troublesome fly, but this time Gordon was more cautious. He neatly dodged the stranger's blow, then swung a vicious right squarely for his adversary's unprotected jaw.

The blow smashed solidly home with all of Gordon's weight behind it. The stranger's jaw buckled and gave beneath that shattering impact. Then abruptly his entire face crumpled into distorted ruin. Gordon staggered back a step in sheer horror at the gruesome result of his blow.

The stranger flung a hand up to his shattered features. When his hand came away again, his whole face came away with it!

Gordon had one horror-stricken glimpse of a featureless blob of rubbery bluish-gray flesh in which fiendish eyes of blue-green fire blazed in malignant fury.

Then the stranger fumbled at his collar, ripping the linen swiftly away. Something lashed out from beneath his throat—a loathsome snake-like object, slender and forked at the end. For one ghastly moment, as the writhing tentacle swung into line with him, Gordon saw its forked ends glow strange fire—one a vivid blue, the other a sparkling green.

Then the world was abruptly blotted out for Blair Gordon.

CONSCIOUSNESS returned to Gordon as swiftly and painlessly as it had left him. For a moment he blinked stupidly in a dazed effort to comprehend the incredible scene before him.

He was seated in a chair over near the wall of a large room that was flooded with livid red light from a single globe overhead. Beside him sat Leah Keith, also staring with dazed eyes in an effort to comprehend her surroundings. Directly in front of them stood a figure of stark nightmare horror.

The weirdly glowing eyes identified the figure as that of the stranger at the Maori Hut, but there every point of resemblance ceased. Only the cleverest of facial masques and body padding could ever have enabled this monstrosity to pass unnoticed in a world of normal human beings.

Now that his disguise was completely stripped away, his slight frame was revealed as a grotesque parody of that of a human being, with arms and legs like pipe-stems, a bald oval head that merged with neckless rigidity directly into a heavy-shouldered body that tapered into an almost wasp-like slenderness at the waist. He was naked save for a loin cloth of some metallic fabric. His bluish-gray skin had a dull oily sheen strangely suggestive of fine grained flexible metal.

The creature's face was hideously unlike anything human. Beneath the glowing eyes was a small circular mouth orifice with a cluster of gill-like appendages on either side of it. Patches of lighter-colored skin on either side of the head seemed to serve as ears. From a point just under the head, where the throat of a human being would have been, dangled the foot-and-a-half long tentacle whose forked tip had sent Gordon into oblivion.

Behind the creature Gordon was dimly aware of a maze of complicated and utterly unfamiliar apparatus ranged along the opposite wall, giving the room the appearance of being a laboratory of some kind.

GORDON'S obvious bewilderment seemed to amuse the bluish-gray monstrosity. "May I introduce myself?" he asked with a mocking note in his metallic voice. "I am Arlok of Xoran. I am an explorer of Space, and more particularly an Opener of Gates. My home is upon Xoran, which is one of the eleven major planets that circle about the giant blue-white sun that your astronomers call Rigel. I am here to open the Gate between your world and mine."

Gordon reached a reassuring hand over to Leah. All memory of their quarrel was obliterated in the face of their present peril. He felt her slender fingers twine firmly with his. The warm contact gave them both new courage.

"We of Xoran need your planet and intend to take possession of it," Arlok continued, "but the vast distance which separates Rigel from your solar system makes it impracticable to transport any considerable number of our people here in space-cars for, though our space-cars travel with practically the speed of light, it requires over five hundred and forty years for them to cross that great void. So I was sent as a lone pioneer to your Earth to do the work necessary here in order to open the Gate that will enable Xoran to cross the barrier in less than a minute of your time.

"THAT gate is the one through the fourth dimension, for Xoran and your planet in a four-dimensional universe are almost touching each other in spite of the great distance separating them in a three-dimensional universe. We of Xoran, being three-dimensional creatures like you Earthlings, can not even exist on a four-dimensional plane. But we can, by the use of apparatus to open a Gate, pass through a thin sector of the fourth dimension and emerge in a far distant part of our three-dimensional universe.

"The situation of our two worlds," Arlok continued, "is somewhat like that of two dots on opposite ends of a long strip of paper that is curved almost into a circle. To two-dimensional beings capable only of realizing and traveling along the two dimensions of the paper itself those dots might be many feet apart, yet in the third dimension straight across free space they might be separated by only the thousandth part of an inch. In order to take that short cut across the third dimension the two-dimensional creatures of the paper would have only to transform a small strip of the intervening space into a two-dimensional surface like their paper.

"They could, do this, of course, by the use of proper vibration-creating machinery, for all things in a material universe are merely a matter of vibration. We of Xoran plan to cross the barrier of the fourth dimension by creating a narrow strip of vibrations powerful enough to exactly match and nullify those of the fourth dimension itself. The result will be that this narrow strip will temporarily become an area of three dimensions only, an area over which we can safely pass from our world to yours."

ARLOK indicated one of the pieces of apparatus along the opposite wall of the room. It was an intricate arrangement of finely wound coils with wires leading to scores of needle-like points which constantly shimmered and crackled with tiny blue-white flames. Thick cables ran to a bank of concave reflectors of some gleaming grayish metal.

"There is the apparatus which will supply the enormous power necessary to nullify the vibrations of the fourth dimensional barrier," Arlok explained. "It is a condenser and adapter of the cosmic force that you call the Millikan rays. In Xoran a similar apparatus is already set up and finished, but the Gate can only be opened by simultaneous actions from both sides of the barrier. That is why I was sent on my long journey through space to do the necessary work here. I am now nearly finished. A very few hours more will see the final opening of the Gate. Then the fighting hordes of Xoran can sweep through the barrier and overwhelm your planet.

"When the Gate from Xoran to a new planet is first opened," Arlok continued, "our scientists always like to have at least one pair of specimens of the new world's inhabitants sent through to them for experimental use. So to-night, while waiting for one of my final castings to cool, I improved the time by making a brief raid upon the place that you call the Maori Hut. The lady here seemed an excellent type of your Earthling women, and the meteoric iron in her necklace made a perfect focus for electric hypnosis. Her escort was too inferior a specimen to be of value to me so I killed him when he attempted to interfere. When you gave chase I lured you on until I could see whether you might be usable. You proved an excellent specimen, so I merely stunned you. Very soon now I shall be ready to send the two of you through the Gate to our scientists in Xoran."

A COLD wave of sheer horror swept over Gordon. It was impossible to doubt the stark and deadly menace promised in the plan of this grim visitor from an alien universe—a menace that loomed not only for Gordon and Leah but for the teeming millions of a doomed and defenseless world.

"Let me show you Xoran," Arlok offered. "Then you may be better able to understand." He turned his back carelessly upon his two captives and strode over to the apparatus along the opposite wall.

Gordon longed to hurl himself upon the unprotected back of the retreating Xoranian, but he knew that any attempt of that kind would be suicidal. Arlok's deadly tentacle would strike him down before he was halfway across the room.

He searched his surroundings with desperate eyes for anything that might serve as a weapon. Then his pulse quickened with sudden hope. There on a small table near Leah was the familiar bulk of a .45 calibre revolver, loaded and ready for use. It was included in a miscellaneous collection of other small earthly tools and objects that Arlok had apparently collected for study.

There was an excellent chance that Leah might be able to secure the gun unobserved. Gordon pressed her fingers in a swift attempt at signalling, then jerked his head ever so slightly toward the table. A moment later the quick answering pressure of Leah's fingers told him that she had understood his message. From the corner of his eye Gordon saw Leah's other hand begin cautiously groping behind her for the revolver.

THEN both Gordon and Leah froze into sudden immobility as Arlok faced them again from beside an apparatus slightly reminiscent of an earthly radio set. Arlok threw a switch, and a small bank of tubes glowed pale green. A yard-square plate of bluish-gray metal on the wall above the apparatus glowed with milky fluorescence.

"It is easy to penetrate the barrier with light waves," Arlok explained. "That is a Gate that can readily be opened from either side. It was through it that we first discovered your Earth."

Arlok threw a rheostat on to more power. The luminous plate cleared swiftly. "And there, Earthlings, is Xoran!" Arlok said proudly.

Leah and Gordon gasped in sheer amaze as the glowing plate became a veritable window into another world—a world of utter and alien terror.

The livid light of a giant red sun blazed mercilessly down upon a landscape from which every vestige of animal and plant life had apparently been stripped. Naked rocks and barren soil stretched illimitably to the far horizon in a vast monotony of utter desolation.

Arlok twirled the knob of the apparatus, and another scene flashed into view. In this scene great gleaming squares and cones of metal rose in towering clusters from the starkly barren land. Hordes of creatures like Arlok swarmed in and around the metal buildings. Giant machines whirled countless wheels in strange tasks. From a thousand great needle-like projections on the buildings spurted shimmering sheets of crackling flame, bathing the entire scene in a whirling mist of fiery vapors.

Gordon realized dimly that he must be looking into one of the cities of Xoran, but every detail of the chaotic whirl of activity was too utterly unfamiliar to carry any real significance to his bewildered brain. He was as hopelessly overwhelmed as an African savage would be if transported suddenly into the heart of Times Square.

ARLOK again twirled the knob. The scene shifted, apparently to another planet. This world was still alive, with rich verdure and swarming millions of people strangely like those of Earth. But it was a doomed world. The dread Gate to Xoran had already been opened here. Legions of bluish-gray Xoranians were attacking the planet's inhabitants, and the attack of those metallic hosts was irresistible.

The slight bodies of the Xoranians seemed as impervious to bullets and missiles as though armor-plated. The frantic defense of the beleaguered people of the doomed planet caused hardly a casualty in the Xoranian ranks.

The attack of the Xoranians was hideously effective. Clouds of dense yellow fog belched from countless projectors in the hands of the bluish-gray hosts, and beneath that deadly miasma all animal and plant life on the doomed planet was crumbling, dying, and rotting into a liquid slime. Then even the slime was swiftly obliterated, and the Xoranians were left triumphant upon a world starkly desolate.

"That was one of the minor planets in the swarm that make up the solar system of the sun that your astronomers call Canopus," Arlok explained. "Our first task in conquering a world is to rid it of the unclean surface scum of animal and plant life. When this noxious surface mold is eliminated, the planet is then ready to furnish us sustenance, for we Xoranians live directly upon the metallic elements of the planet itself. Our bodies are of a substance of which your scientists have never even dreamed—deathless, invincible, living metal!"

ARLOK again twirled the control of the apparatus and the scene was shifted back to the planet of Xoran, this time to the interior of what was apparently a vast laboratory. Here scores of Xoranian scientists were working upon captives who were pathetically like human beings of Earth itself, working with lethal gases and deadly liquids as human scientists might experiment upon noxious pests. The details of the scene were so utterly revolting, the tortures that were being inflicted so starkly horrible, that Leah and Gordon sank back in their chairs sick and shaken.

Arlok snapped off a switch, and the green light in the tubes died. "That last scene was the laboratory to which I shall send you two presently," he said callously as he started back across the room toward them.

Gordon lurched to his feet, his brain a seething whirl of hate in which all thought of caution was gone as he tensed his muscles to hurl himself upon that grim monstrosity from the bleak and desolate realm of Xoran.

Then he felt Leah tugging surreptitiously at his right hand. The next moment the bulk of something cold and hard met his fingers. It was the revolver. Leah had secured it while Arlok was busy with his inter-dimensional televisor.

Arlok was rapidly approaching them. Gordon hoped against hope that the menace of that deadly tentacle might be diverted for the fraction of a second necessary for him to get in a crippling shot. Leah seemed to divine his thought. She suddenly screamed hysterically and flung herself on the floor almost at Arlok's feet.

ARLOK stopped in obvious wonder and bent over Leah. Gordon took instant advantage of the Xoranian's diverted attention. He whipped the revolver from behind him and fired point-blank at Arlok's unprotected head.

The bullet struck squarely, but Arlok was not even staggered. A tiny spot of bluish-gray skin upon his oval skull gleamed faintly for a moment under the bullet's impact. Then the heavy pellet of lead, as thoroughly flattened as though it had struck the triple armor of a battleship, dropped spent and harmless to the floor.

Arlok straightened swiftly. For the moment he seemed to have no thought of retaliating with his deadly tentacle. He merely stood there quite still with one thin arm thrown up to guard his glowing eyes.

Gordon sent the remainder of the revolver's bullets crashing home as fast as his finger could press the trigger. At that murderously short range the smashing rain of lead should have dropped a charging gorilla. But for all the effect Gordon's shots had upon the Xoranian, his ammunition might as well have been pellets of paper. Arlok's glossy hide merely, glowed momentarily in tiny patches as the bullets struck and flattened harmlessly—and that was all.

His last cartridge fired, Gordon flung the empty weapon squarely at the blue monstrosity's hideous face. Arlok made no attempt to dodge. The heavy revolver struck him high on the forehead, then rebounded harmlessly to the floor. Arlok paid no more attention to the blow than a man would to the casual touch of a wind-blown feather.

Gordon desperately flung himself forward upon the Xoranian in one last mad effort to overwhelm him. Arlok dodged Gordon's wild blows, then gently swept the Earth man into the embrace of his thin arms. For one helpless moment Gordon sensed the incredible strength and adamantine hardness of the Xoranian's slender figure, together with an overwhelming impression of colossal weight in that deceptively slight body.

THEN Arlok contemptuously flung Gordon away from him. As Gordon staggered backward, Arlok's tentacle lashed upward and levelled upon him. Its twin tips again glowed brilliant green and livid blue. Instantly every muscle in Gordon's body was paralyzed. He stood there as rigid as a statue, his body completely deadened from the neck down. Beside him stood Leah, also frozen motionless in that same weird power.

"Earthling, you are beginning to try my patience," Arlok snapped. "Can you not realize that I am utterly invincible in any combat with you? The living metal of my body weighs over sixteen hundred pounds, as you measure weight. The strength inherent in that metal is sufficient to tear a hundred of your Earth men to shreds. But I do not even have to touch you to vanquish you. The electric content of my bodily structure is so infinitely superior to yours that with this tentacle-organ of mine I can instantly short-circuit the feeble currents of your nerve impulses and bring either paralysis or death as I choose.

"But enough of this!" Arlok broke off abruptly. "My materials are now ready, and it is time that I finished my work. I shall put you out of my way for a few hours until I am ready to send you through the Gate to the laboratories of Xoran."

The green and blue fire of the tentacle's tips flamed to dazzling brightness. The paralysis of Gordon's body swept swiftly over his brain. Black oblivion engulfed him.

WHEN Gordon again recovered consciousness he found that he was lying on the floor of what was apparently a narrow hall, near the foot of a stairway. His hands were lashed tightly behind him, and his feet and legs were so firmly pinioned together that he could scarcely move.

Beside him lay Leah, also tightly bound. A short distance down the hall was the closed door of Arlok's work-room, recognizable by the thin line of red light gleaming beneath it.

Moonlight through a window at the rear of the hall made objects around Gordon fairly clear. He looked at Leah and saw tears glistening on her long lashes.

"Oh, Blair, I was afraid you'd never waken again," the girl sobbed. "I thought that fiend had killed you!" Her voice broke hysterically.

"Steady, darling," Gordon said soothingly. "We simply can't give up now, you know. If that monstrosity ever opens that accursed Gate of his our entire world is doomed. There must be some way to stop him. We've got to find that way and try it—even if it seems only one forlorn chance in a million."

GORDON shook his head to clear the numbness still lingering from the effect of Arlok's tentacle. The Xoranian seemed unable to produce a paralysis of any great duration with his weird natural weapon. Accordingly, he had been forced to bind his captives like two trussed fowls while he returned to his labors.

Lying close together as they were, it was a comparatively easy matter for them to get their bound hands within reach of each other, but after fifteen minutes of vain work Gordon realized that any attempt at untying the ropes was useless. Arlok's prodigious strength had drawn the knots so tight that no human power could ever loosen them.

Then Gordon suddenly thought of the one thing in his pockets that might help them. It was a tiny cigarette lighter, of the spring-trigger type. It was in his vest pocket completely out of reach of his bound hands, but there was a way out of that difficulty.

Gordon and Leah twisted and rolled their bodies like two contortionists until they succeeded in getting into such a position that Leah was able to get her teeth in the cloth of the vest pocket's edge. A moment of desperate tugging, then the fabric gave way. The lighter dropped from the torn pocket to the floor, where Leah retrieved it.

Then they twisted their bodies back to back. Leah managed to get the lighter flaming in her bound hands. Gordon groped in an effort to guide the ropes on his wrists over the tiny flickering flame.

THEN there came the faint welcome odor of smoldering rope as the lighter's tiny flame bit into the bonds. Gordon bit his lips to suppress a cry of pain as the flame seared into his skin as well. The flame bit deeper into the rope. A single strand snapped.

Then another strand gave way. To Gordon the process seemed endless as the flame scorched rope and flesh alike. A long minute of lancing agony that seemed hours—then Gordon could stand no more. He tensed his muscles in one mighty agonized effort to end the torture of the flame.

The weakened rope gave way completely beneath that pain-maddened lunge. Gordon's hands were free. It was an easy matter now to use the lighter to finish freeing himself and Leah. They made their way swiftly back to the window at the rear of the hall. It slid silently upward. A moment later, and they were out in the brilliant moonlight—free.

They made their way around to the front of the house. Behind the drawn shades of one of the front rooms an eery glow of red light marked the location of Arlok's work-room. They heard the occasional clink of tools inside the room as the Xoranian diligently worked to complete his apparatus.

They crept stealthily up to where one of the French windows of Arlok's work-room swung slightly ajar. Through the narrow crevice they could see Arlok's grotesque back as he labored over the complex assembly of apparatus against the wall.

A heavy stone flung through the window would probably wreck that delicate mechanism completely, yet the two watchers knew that such a respite would be only a temporary one. As long as Arlok remained alive on this planet to build other gates to Xoran, Earth's eventual doom was certain. Complete destruction of Arlok himself was Earth's only hope of salvation.

THE Xoranian seemed to be nearing the end of his labors. He left the apparatus momentarily and walked over to a work-bench where he picked up a slender rod-like tool. Donning a heavy glove to shield his left hand, he selected a small plate of bluish-gray metal, then pressed a switch in the handle of the tool in his right hand.

A blade of blinding white flame, seemingly as solid as a blade of metal, spurted for the length of a foot from the tool's tip. Arlok began cutting the plate with the flame, the blade shearing through the heavy metal as easily as a hot knife shears through butter.

The sight brought a sudden surge of exultant hope to Gordon. He swiftly drew Leah away from the window, far enough to the side that their low-voiced conversation could not be heard from inside the work-room.

"Leah, there is our one chance!" he explained excitedly. "That blue fiend *is* vulnerable, and that flame-tool of his is the weapon to reach his vulnerability. Did you notice how careful he was to shield his other hand with a glove before he turned the tool on? He can be hurt by that blade of flame, and probably hurt badly."

Leah nodded in quick understanding. "If I could lure him out of the room for just a moment, you could slip in through the window and get that flame-tool, Blair," she suggested eagerly.

"That might work," Gordon agreed reluctantly. "But, Leah, don't run any more risks than you absolutely have to!" He picked up a small rock. "Here, take this with you. Open the door into the hall and attract Arlok's attention by throwing the rock at his precious apparatus. Then the minute he sees you, try to escape out through the hall again. He'll leave his work to follow you. When he returns to his work-room I'll be in there waiting for him. And I'll be waiting with a weapon that can stab through even that armor-plated hide of his!"

They separated, Leah to enter the house, Gordon to return to the window.

ARLOK was back over in front of the apparatus, fitting into place the piece of metal he had just cut. The flame-tool, its switch now turned off, was still on the work-bench.

Gordon's heart pounded with excitement as he crouched there with his eyes fixed upon the closed hall door. The minutes seemed to drag interminably. Then suddenly Gordon's muscles tensed. The knob of the hall door had turned ever so slightly. Leah was at her post!

The next moment the door was flung open with a violence that sent it slamming back against the wall. The slender figure of Leah stood framed in the opening, her dark eyes blazing as she flung one hand up to hurl her missile.

Arlok whirled just as Leah threw the rock straight at the intricate Gate-opening apparatus. With the speed of thought the Xoranian flung his own body over to shield his fragile instruments. The rock thudded harmlessly against his metallic chest.

Then Arlok's tentacle flung out like a striking cobra, its forked tip flaming blue and green fire as it focussed upon the open door. But Leah was already gone. Gordon heard her flying footsteps as she raced down the hall. Arlok promptly sped after her in swift pursuit.

As Arlok passed through the door into the hall Gordon flung himself into the room, and sped straight for the work-bench. He snatched the flame-tool up, then darted over to the wall by the door. He was not a second too soon. The heavy tread of Arlok's return was already audible in the hall just outside.

Gordon prepared to stake everything upon his one slim chance of disabling that fearful tentacle before Arlok could bring it into action. He pressed the tiny switch in the flame-tool's handle just as Arlok came through the door.

ARLOK, startled by the glare of the flame-tool's blazing blade, whirled toward Gordon—but too late. That thin searing shaft of vivid flame had already struck squarely at the base of the Xoranian's tentacle. A seething spray of hissing sparks marked the place where the flame bit deeply home. Arlok screamed, a ghastly metallic note of anguish like nothing human.

The Xoranian's powerful hands clutched at Gordon, but he leaped lithely backward out of their reach. Then Gordon again attacked, the flame-tool's shining blade licking in and out like a rapier. The searing flame swept across one of Arlok's arms, and the Xoranian winced. Then the blade stabbed swiftly at Arlok's waist. Arlok half-doubled as he flinched back. Gordon shifted his aim with lightning speed and sent the blade of flame lashing in one accurate terrible stroke that caught Arlok squarely in the eyes.

Again Arlok screamed in intolerable agony as that tearing flame darkened forever his glowing eyes. In berserker fury the tortured Xoranian charged blindly toward Gordon. Gordon warily dodged to one side. Arlok, sightless, and with his tentacle crippled, still had enough power in that mighty metallic body of his to tear a hundred Earth men to pieces.

Gordon stung Arlok's shoulder with the flame, then desperately leaped to one side just in time to dodge a flailing blow that would have made pulp of his body had it landed.

Arlok went stark wild in his frenzied efforts to come to grips with his unseen adversary. Furniture crashed and splintered to kindling wood beneath his threshing feet. Even the stout walls of the room shivered and cracked as the incredible weight of Arlok's body caromed against them.

GORDON circled lithely around the crippled blue monstrosity like a timber wolf circling a wounded moose. He began concentrating his attack upon Arlok's left leg. Half a dozen deep slashes with the searing flame—then suddenly the thin leg crumpled and broke. Arlok crashed helplessly to the floor.

Gordon was now able to shift his attack to Arlok's head. Dodging the blindly flailing arms of the Xoranian, he stabbed again and again at that oval-shaped skull.

The searing thrusts began to have their effect. Arlok's convulsive movements became slower and weaker. Gordon sent the flame stabbing in a long final thrust in an attempt to pierce through to that alien metal brain.

With startling suddenness the flame burned its way home to some unknown center of life force in the oval skull. There was a brief but appalling gush of bright purple flame from Arlok's eye-sockets and mouth orifice. Then his twitching body stiffened. His bluish-gray hide darkened with incredible swiftness into a dull black. Arlok was dead.

Gordon, sickened at the grisly ending to the battle, snapped off the flame-tool and turned to search for Leah. He found her already standing in the hall door, alive, and unhurt.

"I ESCAPED through the window at the end of the hall," she explained. "Arlok quit following me as soon as he saw that you too were gone from where he had left us tied." She shuddered as she looked down at the Xoranian's mangled body. "I saw most of your fight with him, Blair. It was terrible; awful. But, Blair, we've won!"

"Yes, and now we'll make sure of the fruits of our victory," Gordon said grimly, starting over toward the Gate-opening apparatus with the flame-tool in his hand. A very few minutes' work with the shearing blade of flame reduced the intricate apparatus to a mere tangled pile of twisted metal.

Arlok, Gate-opener of Xoran, was dead—and the Gate to that grim planet was now irrevocably closed!

"Blair, do you feel it too, that eery feeling of countless eyes still watching us from Xoran?" There was frank awe in Leah's half-whispered question. "You know Arlok said that they had watched us for centuries from their side of the barrier. I'm sure they're watching us now. Will they send another Opener of Gates to take up the work where Arlok failed?"

Gordon took Leah into his arms. "I don't know, dear," he admitted gravely. "They may send another messenger, but I doubt it. This world of ours has had its warning, and it will heed it. The watchers on Xoran must know that in the five hundred and forty years it would take their next messenger to get here, the Earth will have had more than enough time to prepare an adequate defense for even Xoran's menace. I doubt if there will ever again be an attempt made to open the Gate to Xoran."

The great ship tore apart.

THE EYE OF ALLAH

By C. D. Willard

On the fatal seventh of September a certain Secret Service man sat in the President's chair and—looked back into the Eye of Allah.

Blinky Collins' part in this matter was very brief. Blinky lasted just long enough to make a great discovery, to brag about it as was Blinky's way, and then pass on to find his reward in whatever hereafter is set apart for weak-minded crooks whose heads are not hard enough to withstand the crushing impact of a lead-filled pacifier.

The photograph studio of Blinky Collins was on the third floor of a disreputable building in an equally unsavory part of Chicago. There were no tinted pictures of beautiful blondes nor of stern, square-jawed men of affairs in Blinky's reception room. His clients, who came furtively there, were strongly opposed to having their pictures taken—they came for other purposes. For the photographic work of Mr. Collins was strictly commercial—and peculiar. There were fingerprints to be photographed and identified for purpose of private revenge, photographs of people to be merged and repictured in compromising closeness for reasons of blackmail. And even X-Ray photography was included in the scope of his work.

THE great discovery came when a box was brought to the dingy room and Mr. Collins was asked to show what was inside it without the bother and inconvenience of disturbing lock and seals. The X-Ray machine sizzled above it, and a photographic plate below was developed to show a string of round discs that could easily have been pearls.

The temporary possessor of the box was pleased with the result—but Blinky was puzzled. For the developer had brought out an odd result. There were the pearls as expected, but, too, there was a small picture superimposed—a picture of a bald head and a body beneath seated beside a desk. The picture had been taken from above looking straight down, and head and desk were familiar.

Blinky knew them both. The odd part was that he knew also that both of them were at that instant on the ground floor of the same disreputable building, directly under and two floors below his workshop.

Like many great discoveries, this of Blinky's came as the result of an accident. He had monkeyed with the X-Ray generator and had made certain substitutions. And here was the result—a bald head and a desk, photographed plainly through two heavy wood floors. Blinky scratched his own head in deep thought. And then he repeated the operation.

This time there was a blonde head close to the bald one, and two people were close to the desk and to each other. Blinky knew then that there were financial possibilities in this new line of portrait work.

It was some time before the rat eyes of the inventor were able to see exactly what they wanted through this strange device, but Blinky learned. And he fitted a telescope back of the ray and found that he could look along it and see as if through a great funnel what was transpiring blocks and blocks away; he looked where he would, and brick walls or stone were like glass when the new ray struck through them.

Blinky never knew what he had—never dreamed of the tremendous potentialities in his oscillating ethereal ray that had a range and penetration beyond anything known. But he knew, in a vague way, that this ray was a channel for light waves to follow, and he learned that he could vary the range of the ray and that whatever light was shown at the end of that range came to him as clear and distinct as if he were there in the room.

He sat for hours, staring through the telescope. He would train the device upon a building across the street, then cut down the current until the unseen vibration penetrated inside the building. If there was nothing there of interest he would gradually increase the power, and the ray would extend out and still out into other rooms and beyond them to still others. Blinky had a lot of fun, but he never forgot the practical application of the device—practical, that is, from the distorted viewpoint of a warped mind.

"I'VE heard about your machine," said a pasty-faced man one day, as he sat in Blinky's room, "and I think it's a lot of hooey. But I'd give just one grand to know who is with the district attorney this minute."

"Where is he?" asked Blinky.

"Two blocks down the street, in the station house ... and if Pokey Barnard is with him, the lousy stool-pigeon—"

Blinky paid no attention to the other's opinion of one Pokey Barnard; he was busy with a sputtering blue light and a telescope behind a shield of heavy lead.

"Put your money on the table," he said, finally: "there's the dicks ... and there's Pokey. Take a look—"

It was some few minutes later that Blinky learned of another valuable feature in his ray. He was watching the district attorney when the pasty-faced man brushed against a hanging incandescent light. There was a bit of bare wire exposed, and as it swung into the ray the fuses in the Collins studio blew out instantly.

But the squinting eyes at the telescope had seen something first. They had seen the spare form of the district attorney throw itself from the chair as if it had been dealt a blow—or had received an electric shock.

Blinky put in new fuses—heavier ones—and tried it again on another subject. And again the man at the receiving end got a shot of current that sent him sprawling.

"Now what the devil—" demanded Blinky. He stood off and looked at the machine, the wire with its 110 volts, the invisible ray that was streaming out.

"It's insulated, the machine is," he told his caller, "so the juice won't shoot back if I keep my hands off; but why," he demanded profanely, "don't it short on the first thing it touches?"

HE was picturing vaguely a ray like a big insulated cable, with light and current both traveling along a core at its center, cut off, insulated by the ray, so that only the bare end where the ray stopped could make contact.

"Some more of them damn electrons." he hazarded; then demanded of his caller: "But am I one hell of a smart guy? Or am I?"

There was no denying this fact. The pasty-faced man told Blinky with lurid emphasis just how smart. He had seen with his own eyes and this was too good to keep.

He paid his one grand and departed, first to make certain necessary arrangements for the untimely end of one Pokey Barnard, squealer, louse, et cetera, et cetera, and then to spread the glad news through the underworld of Collins' invention.

That was Blinky's big mistake, as was shown a few days later. Not many had taken seriously the account of the photographer's experiments, but there was one who had, as was evident. A bearded man, whose eyes stared somewhat wildly from beneath a shock of frowzy hair, entered the Collins work-room and locked the door behind him. His English was imperfect, but the heavy automatic in his hand could not be misunderstood. He forced the trembling inventor to give a demonstration, and the visitor's face showed every evidence of delight.

"The cur-rent," he demanded with careful words, "the electreek cur-rent, you shall do also. Yes?"

Again the automatic brought quick assent, and again the visitor showed his complete satisfaction. Showed it by slugging the inventor quietly and efficiently and packing the apparatus in the big suitcase he had brought.

Blinky Collins had been fond of that machine. He had found a form of television with uncounted possibilities, and it had been for him the perfect instrument of a blackmailing Peeping Tom; he had learned the secret of directed wireless transmission of power and had seen it as a means for annoying his enemies. Yet Blinky Collins—the late Blinky Collins—offered no least objection, when the bearded man walked off with the machine. His body, sprawled awkwardly in the corner, was quite dead....

AND now, some two months later, in his Washington office, the Chief of the United States Secret Service pushed a paper across his desk to a waiting man and leaned back in his chair.

"What would you make of that, Del?" he asked.

Robert Delamater reached leisurely for the paper. He regarded it with sleepy, half-closed eyes.

There was a crude drawing of an eye at the top. Below was printed—not written—a message in careful, precise letters: "Take warning. The Eye of Allah is upon you. You shall instructions receive from time to time. Follow them. Obey."

Delamater laughed. "Why ask me what I think of a nut letter like that. You've had plenty of them just as crazy."

"This didn't come to me," said the Chief; "it was addressed to the President of the United States."

"Well, there will be others, and we will run the poor sap down. Nothing out of the ordinary I should say."

"That is what I thought—at first. Read this—" The big, heavy-set man pushed another and similar paper across the desk. "This one was addressed to the Secretary of State."

Delamater did not read it at once. He held both papers to the light; his fingers touched the edges only.

"No watermark," he mused; "ordinary white writing stock—sold in all the five and ten cent stores. Tried these for fingerprints I suppose?".

"Read it," suggested the Chief.

"Another picture of an eye," said Delamater aloud, and read: "'Warning. You are dealing with an emissary from a foreign power who is an unfriend of my country. See him no more. This is the first and last warning. The Eye of Allah watches.'

"And what is this below—? 'He did not care for your cigars, Mr. Secretary. Next time—but there must be no next time.'"

DELAMATER read slowly—lazily. He seemed only slightly interested except when he came to the odd conclusion of the note. But the Chief knew Delamater and knew how that slow indolence could give place to a feverish, alert concentration when work was to be done.

"Crazy as a loon," was the man's conclusion as he dropped the papers upon the desk.

"Crazy," his chief corrected, "like a fox! Read the last line again; then get this—

"The Secretary of State *is* meeting with a foreign agent who is here very much incog. Came in as a servant of a real ambassador. Slipped quietly into Washington, and not a soul knew he was here. He met the Secretary in a closed room; no one saw him come or leave—";

"Well, the Secretary tells me that in that room where nobody could see he offered this man a cigar. His visitor took it, tried to smoke it, apologized—and lit one of his own vile cigarettes."

"Hm-m!" Delamater sat a little straighter in his chair; his eyebrows were raised now in questioning astonishment. "Dictaphone? Some employee of the Department listening in?"

"Impossible."

"Now that begins to be interesting," the other conceded. His eyes had lost their sleepy look. "Want me to take it on?"

"Later. Right now. I want you to take this visiting gentleman under your personal charge. Here is the name and the room and hotel where he is staying. He is to meet with the Secretary to-night—he knows where. You will get to him unobserved—absolutely unseen; I can leave that to you. Take him yourself to his appointment, and take him without a brass band. But have what men you want tail you and watch out for spies.... Then, when he is through, bring him back and deliver him safely to his room. Compray?"

"Right—give me Wilkins and Smeed. I rather think I can get this bird there and back without being seen, but perhaps they may catch Allah keeping tabs on us at that." He laughed amusedly as he took the paper with the name and address.

A WAITER with pencil and order-pad might have been seen some hours later going as if from the kitchen to the ninth floor of a Washington hotel. And the same waiter, a few minutes later, was escorting a guest from a rear service-door to an inconspicuous car parked nearby. The waiter slipped behind the wheel.

A taxi, whose driver was half asleep, was parked a hundred feet behind them at the curb. As they drove away and no other sign of life was seen in the quiet street the driver of the taxi yawned ostentatiously and decided to seek a new stand. He neglected possible fares until a man he called Smeed hailed him a block farther on. They followed slowly after the first car ... and they trailed it again on its return after some hours.

"Safe as a church," they reported to the driver of the first car. "We'll swear that nobody was checking up on that trip."

And: "O. K." Delamater reported to his chief the next morning. "Put one over on this self-appointed Allah that time."

But the Chief did not reply: he was looking at a slip of paper like those he had shown his operative the day before. He tossed it to Delamater and took up the phone.

"To the Secretary of State," Delamater read. "You had your warning. Next time you disobey it shall be you who dies."

The signature was only the image of an eye.

THE Chief was calling a number; Delamater recognized it as that of the hotel he had visited. "Manager, please, at once," the big man was saying.

He identified himself to the distant man. Then: "Please check up on the man in nine four seven. If he doesn't answer, enter the room and report at once—I will hold the phone...."

The man at the desk tapped steadily with a pencil; Robert Delamater sat quietly, tensely waiting. But some sixth sense told him what the answer would be. He was not surprised when the Chief repeated what the phone had whispered.

"Dead?... Yes!... Leave everything absolutely undisturbed. We will be right over."

"Get Doctor Brooks, Del," he said quietly; "the Eye of Allah was watching after all."

Robert Delamater was silent as they drove to the hotel. Where had he slipped? He trusted Smeed and Wilkins entirely; if they said his car had not been followed it had not. And the visitor had been disguised; he had seen to that. Then, where had this person stood—this being who called himself the Eye of Allah?

"Chief," he said finally. "I didn't slip—nor Wilkins or Smeed."

"Someone did," replied the big man, "and it wasn't the Eye of Allah, either."

The manager of the hotel was waiting to take them to the room. He unlocked the door with his pass key.

"Not a thing touched," he assured the Secret Service men; "there he is, just the way we found him."

In the doorway between the bedroom and bath a body was huddled. Doctor Brooks knelt quickly beside it. His hands worked swiftly for a moment, then he rose to his feet.

"Dead," he announced.

"How long?" asked the Chief.

"Some time. Hours I should say—perhaps eight or ten."

"Cause?" the query was brief.

"It will take an autopsy to determine that. There is no blood or wound to be seen."

THE doctor was again examining the partly rigid body. He opened one hand; it held a cake of soap. There was a grease mark on the hand.

Delamater supplied the explanation. "He touched some grease on the old car I was using," he said. "Must have gone directly to wash it off. See—there is water spilled on the floor."

Water had indeed been splashed on the tile floor of the bath room; a pool of it still remained about the heavy, foreign-looking shoes of the dead man.

Something in it caught Delamater's eye. He leaned down to pick up three pellets of metal, like small shot, round and shining.

"I'll keep these," he said, "though the man was never killed with shot as small as that."

"We shall have to wait for the autopsy report," said the Chief crisply; "that may give the cause of death. Was there anyone in the room—did you enter it with him last night, Del?"

"No," said the operative; "he was very much agitated when we got here—dismissed me rather curtly at the door. He was quite upset about something—spoke English none too well and said something about a warning and damned our Secret Service as inefficient."

"A warning!" said the Chief. The dead man's brief case was on the bed. He crossed to it and undid the straps; the topmost paper told the reason for the man's disquiet. It showed the familiar, staring eye. And beneath the eye was a warning: this man was to die if he did not leave Washington at once.

The Chief turned to the hotel manager. "Was the door locked?"

"Yes."

"But it is a spring lock. Someone could have gone out and closed it after him."

"Not this time. The dead-bolt was thrown. It takes a key to do that from the outside or this thumb-turn on the inside." The hotel man demonstrated the action of the heavy bolt.

"Then, with a duplicate key, a man could have left this room and locked the door behind him."

"Absolutely not. The floor-clerk was on duty all night. I have questioned her: this room was under her eyes all the time. She saw this man return, saw your man, here"—and he pointed to Delamater—"leave him at the door. There was no person left the room after that."

"See about the autopsy, Doctor," the Chief ordered.

And to the manager: "Not a thing here must be touched. Admit only Mr. Delamater and no one else unless he vouches for them.

"Del," he told the operative, "I'm giving you a chance to make up for last night. Go to it."

And Robert Delamater "went to it" with all the thoroughness at his command, and with a total lack of result.

THE autopsy helped not at all. The man was dead; it was apparently a natural death. "Not a scratch nor a mark on him," was the report. But: "... next time it will be you," the note with the staring eye had warned the Secretary of State. The writer of it was taking full credit for the mysterious death.

Robert Delamater had three small bits of metal, like tiny shot, and he racked his brain to connect these with the death. There were fingerprints, too, beautifully developed upon the mysterious missives—prints that tallied with none in the records. There were analyses of the paper—of the ink—and not a clue in any of them.

Just three pellets of metal. Robert Delamater had failed utterly, and he was bitter in the knowledge of his failure.

"He had you spotted, Del," the Chief insisted. "The writer of these notes may be crazy, but he was clever enough to know that this man *did* see the Secretary. And he was waiting for him when he came back; then he killed him."

"Without a mark?"

"He killed him," the Chief repeated; "then he left—and that's that."

"But," Delamater objected, "the room clerk—"

"—took a nap," broke in the Chief. But Delamater could not be satisfied with the explanation.

"He got his, all right," he conceded, "—got it in a locked room nine stories above the street, with no possible means of bringing it upon himself—and no way for the murderer to escape. I tell you there is something more to this: just the letter to the Secretary, as if this Eye of Allah were spying upon him—"

The Chief waved all that aside. "A clever spy," he insisted. "Too clever for you. And a darn good guesser; he had us all fooled. But we're dealing with a madman, not a ghost, and he didn't sail in through a ninth story window nor go out through a locked door; neither did he spy on the Secretary of State in his private office. Don't try to make a supernatural mystery out of a failure, Del."

The big man's words were tempered with a laugh, but there was an edge of sarcasm, ill-concealed.

AND then came the next note. And the next. The letters were mailed at various points in and about the city; they came in a flood. And they were addressed to the President of the United States, to the Secretary of War—of the Navy—to all the Cabinet members. And all carried the same threat under the staring eye.

The United States, to this man, represented all that was tyrannical and oppressive to the downtrodden of the earth. He proposed to end it—this government first, then others in their turn. It was the outpouring of a wildly irrational mind that came to the office of the harassed Chief of the United States Secret Service, who had instructions to run this man down—this man who signed himself The Eye of Allah. And do it quickly for the notes were threatening. Official Washington, it seemed, was getting jumpy and was making caustic inquiries as to why a Secret Service department was maintained.

The Chief, himself, was directing the investigation—and getting nowhere.

"Here is the latest," he said one morning. "Mailed at New York." Delamater and a dozen other operatives were in his office: he showed them a letter printed like all the others. There was the eye, and beneath were words that made the readers catch their breath.

"The Eye of Allah sees—it has warned—now it will destroy. The day of judgment is at hand. The battleship *Maryland* is at anchor in the Hudson River at New York. No more shall it be the weapon of a despot government. It will be destroyed at twelve o'clock on September fifth."

"Wild talk," said the Chief, "but today is the fourth. The Commander of the *Maryland* has been warned—approach by air or water will be impossible. I want you men to patrol the shore and nail this man if he shows up. Lord knows what he intends—bluffing probably—but he may try some fool stunt. If he does—get him!"

ELEVEN-THIRTY by the watch on Robert Delamater's wrist found him seated in the bow of a speed-boat the following morning. They patrolled slowly up and down the shore. There were fellow operatives, he knew, scores of them, posted at all points of vantage along the docks.

Eleven forty-five—and the roar of seaplanes came from above where air patrols were-guarding the skies. Small boats drove back and forth on set courses; no curious sight-seeing craft could approach the *Maryland* that day. On board the battleship, too, there was activity apparent. A bugle sounded, and the warning of bellowing Klaxons echoed across the water. Here, in the peace and safety of the big port, the great man-of-war was sounding general quarters, and a scurry of running men showed for an instant on her decks. Anti-aircraft guns swung silently upon imaginary targets—

The watcher smiled at the absurdity of it all—this preparation to repel the attack of a wild-eyed writer of insane threats. And yet—and yet— He knew, too, there was apprehension in his frequent glances at his watch.

One minute to go! Delamater should have watched the shore. And, instead, he could not keep his eyes from the big fighting-ship silhouetted so clearly less than a mile away, motionless and waiting—waiting—for what? He saw the great turreted guns, useless against this puny, invisible opponent. Above them the fighting tops were gleaming. And above them—

Delamater shaded his eyes with a quick, tense hand: the tip of the mast was sparkling. There was a blue flash that glinted along the steel. It was gone to reappear on the fighting top itself—then lower.

WHAT was it? the watching man was asking himself. What did it bring to mind? A street-car? A defective trolley? The zipping flash of a contact made and broken? That last!

Like the touch of a invisible wire, tremendously charged, a wire that touched and retreated, that made and lost its contact, the flashing arc was working toward the deck. It felt its way to the body of the ship; the arc was plain, starting from mid-air to hiss against the armored side; the arc shortened—went to nothing—vanished.... A puff of smoke from an open port proved its presence inside. Delamater had the conviction that a deadly something had gone through the ship's side—was insulated from it—was searching with its blazing, arcing end for the ammunition rooms....

The realization of that creeping menace came to Delamater with a gripping, numbing horror. The seconds were almost endless as he waited. Slowly, before his terrified eyes, the deck of the great ship bulged upward ... slowly it rolled and tore apart ... a mammoth turret with sixteen-inch guns was lifting unhurriedly into the air ... there were bodies of men rocketing skyward....

The mind of the man was racing at lightning speed, and the havoc before him seemed more horrible in its slow, leisurely progress. If he could only move—do something!

The shock of the blasted air struck him sprawling into the bottom of the boat; the listener was hammered almost to numbness by the deafening thunder that battered and tore through the still air. At top speed the helmsman drove for the shelter of a hidden cove. They made it an instant before the great waves struck high upon the sand spit. Over the bay hung a ballooning cloud of black and gray—lifting for an instant to show in stark ghastliness the wreckage, broken and twisted, that marked where the battleship *Maryland* rested in the mud in the harbor of New York.

THE eyes of the Secret-Service men were filled with the indelible impress of what they had seen. Again and again, before him, came the vision of a ship full of men in horrible, slow disintegration; his mind was numbed and his actions and reactions were largely automatic. But somehow he found himself in the roar of the subway, and later he sat in a chair and knew he was in a Pullman of a Washington train.

He rode for hours in preoccupied silence, his gaze fixed unseeingly, striving to reach out and out to some distant, unknown something which he was trying to visualize. But he looked at intervals at his hand that held three metal pellets.

He was groping for the mental sequence which would bring the few known facts together and indicate their cause. A threat—a seeming spying within a closed and secret room—the murder on the ninth floor, a murder without trace of wound or weapon. Weapon! He stared again at the tangible evidence he held; then shook his head in perplexed abstraction. No—the man was killed by unknown means.

And now—the *Maryland*! And a visible finger of death—touching, flashing, feeling its way to the deadly cargo of powder sacks.

Not till he sat alone with his chief did he put into words his thoughts.

"A time bomb did it," the Chief was saying. "The officials deny it, but what other answer is there? No one approached that ship—you know that, Del—no torpedo nor aerial bomb! Nothing as fanciful as that!"

Robert Delamater's lips formed a wry smile. "Nothing at fanciful as that"—and he was thinking, thinking—of what he hardly dared express.

"We will start with the ship's personnel," the other continued; "find every man who was not on board when the explosion occurred—"

"No use," the operative interrupted; "this was no inside job, Chief." He paused to choose his words while the other watched him curiously.

"Someone *did* reach that ship—reached it from a distance—reached it in the same way they reached that poor devil I left at room nine forty-seven. Listen—"

HE told his superior of his vigil on the speed-boat—of the almost invisible flash against the ship's mast. "He reached it, Chief," he concluded; "he felt or saw his way down and through the side of that ship. And he fired their ammunition from God knows where."

"I wonder," said the big man slowly; "I wonder if you know just what you are trying to tell me—just how absurd your idea is. Are you seriously hinting at long-distance vision through solid armor-plate—through these walls of stone and steel? And wireless power-transmission through the same wall—!"

"Exactly!" said the operative.

"Why, Del, you must be as crazy as this Eye of Allah individual. It's impossible."

"That word," said Delamater, quietly, "has been crossed out of scientific books in the past few years."

"What do you mean?"

"You have studied some physical science, of course?" Delamater asked. The Chief nodded.

"Then you know what I mean. I mean that up to recent years science had all the possibilities and impossibilities neatly divided and catalogued. Ignorance, as always, was the best basis for positive assurance. Then they got inside the atom. And since then your real scientist has been a very humble man. He has seen the impossibility of yesterday become the established fact of to-day."

The Chief of the United States Secret Service was tapping with nervous irritation on the desk before him.

"Yes, yes!" he agreed, and again he looked oddly at his operative. "Perhaps there is something to that; you work along that line, Del: you can have a free hand. Take a few days off, a little vacation if you wish. Yes—and ask Sprague to step in from the other office; he has the personnel list."

ROBERT DELAMATER felt the other's eyes follow him as he left the room. "And that about lets me out," he told himself; "he thinks I've gone cuckoo, now."

He stopped in a corridor; his fingers, fumbling in a vest pocket, had touched the little metal spheres. Again his mind flashed back to the chain of events he had linked together. He turned toward an inner office.

"I would like to see Doctor Brooks," he said. And when the physician appeared: "About that man who was murdered at the hotel, Doctor—"

"Who died," the doctor corrected; "we found no evidence of murder."

"Who was murdered," the operative insisted. "Have you his clothing where I can examine it?"

"Sure," agreed the physician. He led Delamater to another room and brought out a box of the dead man's effects.

"But if it's murder you expect to prove you'll find no help in this."

The Secret Service man nodded. "I'll look them over, just the same," he said. "Thanks."

Alone in the room, he went over the clothing piece by piece. Again he examined each garment, each pocket, the lining, as he had done before when first he took the case. Metal, he thought, he must find metal.

But only when a heavy shoe was in his hands did the anxious frown relax from about his eyes.

"Of course," he whispered, half aloud. "What a fool I was! I should have thought of that."

The soles of the shoes were sewed, but, beside the stitches were metal specks, where cobbler's nails were driven. And in the sole of one shoe were three tiny holes.

"Melted!" he said exultantly. "Crazy, am I, Chief? This man was standing on a wet floor; he made a perfect ground. And he got a jolt that melted these nails when it flashed out of him."

He wrapped the clothing carefully and replaced it in the box. And he fingered the metal pellets in his pocket as he slipped quietly from the room.

HE did not stop to talk with Doctor Brooks; he wanted to think, to ponder upon the incredible proof of the theory he had hardly dared believe. The Eye of Allah—the maniac—was real; and his power for evil! There was work to be done, and the point of beginning was not plain.

How far did the invisible arm reach? How far could the Eye of Allah see? Where was the generator—the origin of this wireless power; along what channel did it flow? A ray of lightless light—an unseen ethereal vibration.... Delamater could only guess at the answers.

The current to kill a man or to flash a spark into silken powder bags need not be heavy, he knew. Five hundred—a thousand volts—if the mysterious conductor carried it without resistance and without loss. People had been killed by house-lighting currents—a mere 110 volts—when conditions were right. There would be no peculiar or unusual demand upon the power company to point him toward the hidden maniac.

He tossed restlessly throughout the night, and morning brought no answer to his repeated questions. But it brought a hurry call from his Chief.

"Right away," was the instruction; "don't lose a minute. Come to the office."

He found the big man at his desk. He was quiet, unhurried, but the operative knew at a glance the tense repression that was being exercised—the iron control of nerves that demanded action and found incompetence and helplessness instead.

"I don't believe your fantastic theories," he told Delamater. "Impractical—impossible! But—" He handed the waiting man a paper. "We must not leave a stone unturned."

Delamater said nothing; he looked at the paper in his hand. "To the President of the United States," he read. "Prepare to meet your God. Friday. The eighth. Twelve o'clock."

The signature he hardly saw; the staring, open eye was all too familiar.

"That is to-morrow," said Delamater softly. "The President dies to-morrow."

"NO!" exploded the Chief. "Do you realize what that means? The President murdered—more killings to follow—and the killer unknown! Why the country will be in a panic: the whole structure of the Government is threatened!"

He paused, then added as he struck his open hand upon the desk: "I will have every available man at the White House."

"For witnesses?" asked Delamater coldly.

The big man stared at his operative; the lines of his face were sagging.

"Do you believe—really—he can strike him down—at his desk—from a distance?"

"I know it." Delamater's fingers played for a moment with three bits of metal in his pocket. Unconsciously he voiced his thoughts: "Does the President have nails in his shoes, I wonder?"

"What—what's that?" the Chief demanded.

But Delamater made no reply. He was picturing the President. He would be seated at his desk, waiting, waiting … and the bells would be ringing and whistles blowing from distant shops when the bolt would strike…. It would flash from his feet … through the thick rug … through the rug…. It would have to ground.

He paid no heed to his Chief's repeated question. He was seeing, not the rug in the Presidential office, but below it—underneath it—a heavy pad of rubber.

"If he can be insulated—" he said aloud, and stared unseeingly at his eagerly listening superiors—"even the telephone cut—no possible connection with the ground—"

"For God's sake, Del, if you've got an idea—any hope at all! I'm—I'm up against it, Del."

The operative brought his distant gaze back to the room and the man across from him. "Yes," he said slowly, thoughtfully, "I've got the beginning of an idea; I don't see the end of it yet.

"We can cut him off from the ground—the President, I mean—make an insulated island where he sits. But this devil will get him the instant he leaves ... unless ... unless...."

"Yes—yes?" The Chief's voice was high-pitched with anxious impatience; for the first time he was admitting to himself his complete helplessness in this emergency.

"Unless," said Delamater, as the idea grew and took shape, "unless that wireless channel works both ways. If it does ... if it does...."

The big man made a gesture of complete incomprehension.

"Wait!" said Robert Delamater, sharply. If ever his sleepy indolence had misled his Chief, there was none to do so now in the voice that rang like cold steel. His eyes were slits under the deep-drawn brows, and his mouth was one straight line.

TO the hunter there is no greater game than man. And Robert Delamater, man-hunter, had his treacherous quarry in sight. He fired staccato questions at his Chief.

"Is the President at his desk at twelve?"

"Yes."

"Does he know—about this?"

"Yes."

"Does he know it means death?"

The Chief nodded.

"I see a way—a chance," said the operative. "Do I get a free hand?"

"Yes—Good Lord, yes! If there's any chance of—"

Delamater silenced him. "I'll be the one to take the chance," he said grimly. "Chief, I intend to impersonate the President."

"Now listen— The President and I are about the same build. I know a man who can take care of the make-up; he will get me by anything but a close inspection. This Eye of Allah, up to now, has worked only in the light. We'll have to gamble on that and work our change in the dark.

"The President must go to bed as usual—impress upon him that he may be under constant surveillance. Then, in the night, he leaves—

"Oh, I know he won't want to hide himself, but he must. That's up to you.

"Arrange for me to go to his room before daylight. From that minute on I am the President. Get me his routine for that morning; I must follow it so as to arouse no least suspicion."

"BUT I don't see—" began the Chief. "You will impersonate him—yes—but what then? You will be killed if this maniac makes good. Is the President of the United States to be a fugitive? Is—"

"Hold on, hold on!" said Delamater. He leaned back in his chair; his face relaxed to a smile, then a laugh.

"I've got it all now. Perhaps it will work. If not—" A shrug of the shoulders completed the thought. "And I have been shooting it to you pretty fast haven't I! Now here is the idea—

"I must be in the President's chair at noon. This Allah person will be watching in, so I must be acting the part all morning. I will have the heaviest insulation I can get under the rug, and I'll have something to take the shot instead of myself. And perhaps, perhaps I will send a message back to the Eye of Allah that will be a surprise.

"Is it a bet?" he asked. "Remember, I'm taking the chance—unless you know some better way—"

The Chief's chair came down with a bang. "We'll gamble on it, Del," he said; "we've got to—there is no other way…. And now what do you want?"

"A note to the White House electrician," said Robert Delamater, "and full authority to ask for anything I may need, from the U. S. Treasury down to a pair of wire-cutters."

His smile had become contagious; the Chief's anxious look relaxed. "If you pull this off, Del, they may give you the Treasury or the Mint at that. But remember, republics are notoriously ungenerous."

"We'll have to gamble on that, too," said Robert Delamater.

THE heart of the Nation is Washington. Some, there are, who would have us feel that New York rules our lives. Chicago—San Francisco—these and other great cities sometimes forget that they are mere ganglia on the financial and commercial nervous system. The heart is Washington, and, Congress to the contrary notwithstanding, the heart of that heart is not the domed building at the head of Pennsylvania Avenue, but an American home. A simple, gracious mansion, standing in quiet dignity and whiteness above its velvet lawns.

It is the White House that draws most strongly at the interest and curiosity of the homely, common throng that visits the capital.

But there were no casual visitors at the White House on the seventh of September. Certain Senators, even, were denied admittance. The President was seeing only the members of the Cabinet and some few others.

It is given to a Secret Service operative, in his time, to play many parts. But even a versatile actor might pause at impersonating a President. Robert Delamater was acting the role with never a fumble. He sat, this new Robert Delamater, so startlingly like the Chief Executive, in the chair by a flat top desk. And he worked diligently at a mass of correspondence.

Secretaries came and went; files were brought. Occasionally he replied to a telephone call—or perhaps called someone. It would be hard to say which happened, for no telephone bells rang.

On the desk was a schedule that Delamater consulted. So much time for correspondence—so many minutes for a conference with this or that official, men who were warned to play up to this new Chief Executive as if the life of their real President were at stake.

TO any observer the busy routine of the morning must have passed with never a break. And there was an observer, as Delamater knew. He had wondered if the mystic ray might carry electrons that would prove its presence. And now he knew.

The Chief of the U. S. Secret Service had come for a consultation with the President. And whatever lingering doubts may have stifled his reluctant imagination were dispelled when the figure at the desk opened a drawer.

"Notice this," he told the Chief as he appeared to search for a paper in the desk. "An electroscope; I put it in here last night. It is discharging. The ray has been on since nine-thirty. No current to electrocute me—just a penetrating ray."

He returned the paper to the drawer and closed it.

"So that is that," he said, and picked up a document to which he called the visitor's attention.

"Just acting," he explained. "The audience may be critical; we must try to give them a good show! And now give me a report. What are you doing? Has anything else turned up? I am counting on you to stand by and see that that electrician is on his toes at twelve o'clock."

"Stand by is right," the Chief agreed; "that's about all we can do. I have twenty men in and about the grounds—there will be as many more later on. And I know now just how little use we are to you, Del."

"Your expression!" warned Delamater. "Remember you are talking to the President. Very official and all that."

"Right! But now tell me what is the game, Del. If that devil fails to knock you out here where you are safe, he will get you when you leave the room."

"Perhaps," agreed the pseudo-executive, "and again, perhaps not. He won't get me here; I am sure of that. They have this part of the room insulated. The phone wire is cut—my conversations there are all faked.

"There is only one spot in this room where that current can pass. A heavy cable is grounded outside in wet earth. It comes to a copper plate on this desk; you can't see it—it is under those papers."

"AND if the current comes—" began the visitor.

"When it comes," the other corrected, "it will jump to that plate and go off harmlessly—I hope."

"And then what? How does that let you out?"

"Then we will see," said the presidential figure. "And you've been here long enough, Chief. Send in the President's secretary as you go out."

"He arose to place a friendly, patronizing hand on the other's shoulder.

"Good-by," he said, "and watch that electrician at twelve. He is to throw the big switch when I call."

"Good luck," said the big man huskily. "We've got to hand it to you, Del; you're—"

"Good-by!" The figure of the Chief Executive turned abruptly to his desk.

There was more careful acting—another conference—some dictating. The clock on the desk gave the time as eleven fifty-five. The man before the flat topped desk verified it by a surreptitious glance at his watch. He dismissed the secretary and busied himself with some personal writing.

Eleven fifty-nine—and he pushed paper and pen aside. The movement disturbed some other papers, neatly stacked. They were dislodged, and where they had lain was a disk of dull copper.

"Ready," the man called softly. "Don't stand too near that line." The first boom of noonday bells came faintly to the room.

The President—to all but the other actors in the morning's drama—leaned far back in his chair. The room was suddenly deathly still. The faint ticking of the desk clock was loud and rasping. There was heavy breathing audible in the room beyond. The last noonday chime had died away....

The man at the desk was waiting—waiting. And he thought he was prepared, nerves steeled, for the expected. But he jerked back, to fall with the overturned chair upon the soft, thick-padded rug, at the ripping, crackling hiss that tore through the silent room.

FROM a point above the desk a blue arc flamed and wavered. Its unseen terminal moved erratically in the air, but the other end of the deadly flame held steady upon a glowing, copper disc.

Delamater, prone on the floor, saw the wavering point that marked the end of the invisible carrier of the current—saw it drift aside till the blue arc was broken. It returned, and the arc crashed again into blinding flame. Then, as abruptly, the blue menace vanished.

The man on the floor waited, waited, and tried to hold fast to some sense of time.

Then: "Contact!" he shouted. "The switch! Close the switch!"

"Closed!" came the answer from a distant room. There was a shouted warning to unseen men: "Stand back there—back—there's twenty thousand volts on that line—"

Again the silence....

"Would it work? Would it?" Delamater's mind was full of delirious, half-thought hopes. That fiend in some far-off room had cut the current meant as a death-bolt to the Nation's' head. He would leave the ray on—look along it to gloat over his easy victory. His generator must be insulated: would he touch it with his hand, now that his own current was off?—make of himself a conductor?

In the air overhead formed a terrible arc.

From the floor, Delamater saw it rip crashingly into life as twenty thousand volts bridged the gap of a foot or less to the invisible ray. It hissed tremendously in the stillness....

And Delamater suddenly buried his face in his hands. For in his mind he was seeing a rigid, searing body, and in his nostrils, acrid, distinct, was the smell of burning flesh.

"Don't be a fool," he told himself fiercely. "Don't be a fool! Imagination!"

The light was out.

"Switch off!" a voice was calling. There was a rush of swift feet from the distant doors; friendly hands were under him—lifting him—as the room, for Robert Delamater, President-in-name of the United States, turned whirlingly, dizzily black....

ROBERT DELAMATER, U. S. Secret Service operative, entered the office of his Chief. Two days of enforced idleness and quiet had been all he could stand. He laid a folded newspaper before the smiling, welcoming man.

"That's it, I suppose," he said, and pointed to a short notice.

"X-ray Operator Killed," was the caption. "Found Dead in Office in Watts Building." He had read the brief item many times.

"That's what we let the reporters have," said the Chief.

"Was he"—the operative hesitated for a moment—"pretty well fried?"

"Quite!"

"And the machine?"

"Broken glass and melted metal. He smashed it as he fell."

"The Eye of Allah," mused Delamater. "Poor devil—poor, crazy devil. Well, we gambled—and we won. How about the rest of the bet? Do I get the Mint?"

"Hell, no!" said the Chief. "Do you expect to win all the time? They want to know why it took us so long to get him.

"Now, there's a little matter out in Ohio, Del, that we'll have to get after—"

THE "TELELUX"

SOUND and light were transformed into mechanical action at the banquet of the National Tool Exposition recently to illustrate their possibilities in regulating traffic, aiding the aviator, and performing other automatic functions.

A beam of light was thrown on the "eyes" of a mechanical contrivance known as the "telelux," a brother of the "televox," and as the light was thrown on and off it performed mechanical function such as turning an electric switch.

The contrivance, which was developed by the Westinghouse Electric and Manufacturing Company, utilizes two photo-electric cells, sensitive to the light beam. One of the cells is a selector, which progressively chooses any one of three operating circuits when light is thrown on it. The other cell is the operator, which opens or closes the chosen circuit, thus performing the desired function.

S. M. Kintner, manager of the company's research department, who made the demonstration, also threw music across the room on a beam of light, and light was utilized in depicting the shape and direction of stresses in mechanical materials.

"The globe leaped upward into the huge coil, which whirled madly."

THE FIFTH-DIMENSION CATAPULT

A COMPLETE NOVELETTE

By Murray Leinster

The story of Tommy Reames' extraordinary rescue of Professor Denham and his daughter—marooned in the fifth dimension.

FOREWORD

THIS story has no normal starting-place, because there are too many places where it might be said to begin. One might commence when Professor Denham, Ph. D., M. A., etc., isolated a metal that scientists have been talking about for many years without ever being able to smelt. Or it might start with his first experimental use of that metal with entirely impossible results. Or it might very plausibly begin with an interview between a celebrated leader of gangsters in the city of Chicago and a spectacled young laboratory assistant, who had turned over to him a peculiar heavy object of solid gold and very nervously explained, and finally managed to prove, where it came from. With also impossible results, because it turned "King" Jacaro, lord of vice-resorts and rum-runners, into a passionate enthusiast in non-Euclidean geometry. The whole story might be said to begin with the moment of that interview.

But that leaves out Smithers, and especially it leaves out Tommy Reames. So, on the whole, it is best to take up the narrative at the moment of Tommy's first entrance into the course of events.

CHAPTER I

HE came to a stop in a cloud of dust that swirled up to and all about the big roadster, and surveyed the gate of the private road. The gate was rather impressive. At its top was a sign. "Keep Out!" Halfway down was another sign. "Private Property. Trespassers Will Be Prosecuted." On one gate-post was another notice, "Live Wires Within." and on the other a defiant placard. "Savage Dogs At Large Within This Fence."

The fence itself was all of seven feet high and made of the heaviest of woven-wire construction. It was topped with barbed wire, and went all the way down both sides of a narrow right of way until it vanished in the distance.

Tommy got out of the car and opened the gate. This fitted the description of his destination, as given him by a brawny, red-headed filling-station attendant in the village some two miles back. He drove the roadster through the gate, got out and closed it piously, got back in the car and shot it ahead.

He went humming down the narrow private road at forty-five miles an hour. That was Tommy Reames' way. He looked totally unlike the conventional description of a scientist of any sort—as much unlike a scientist as his sport roadster looked unlike a scientist's customary means of transit—and ordinarily he acted quite unlike one. As a matter of fact, most of the people Tommy associated with had no faintest inkling of his taste for science as an avocation. There was Peter Dalzell, for instance, who would have held up his hands in holy horror at the idea of Tommy Reames being the author of that article. "On the Mass and Inertia of the Tesseract," which in the *Philosophical Journal* had caused a controversy.

And there was one Mildred Holmes—of no importance in the matter of the Fifth-Dimension Catapult—who would have lifted beautifully arched eyebrows in bored unbelief if anybody had suggested that Tommy Reames was that Thomas Reames whose "Additions to Herglotz's Mechanics of Continua" produced such diversities of opinion in scientific circles. She intended to make Tommy propose to her some day, and thought she knew all about him. And everybody, everywhere, would have been incredulous of his present errand.

GLIDING down the narrow, fenced-in road. Tommy was a trifle dubious about this errand himself. A yellow telegraph-form in his pocket read rather like a hoax, but was just plausible enough to have brought him away from a rather important tennis match. The telegram read:

PROFESSOR DENHAM IN EXTREME DANGER THROUGH EXPERIMENT BASED ON YOUR ARTICLE ON DOMINANT COORDINATES YOU ALONE CAN HELP HIM IN THE NAME OF HUMANITY COME AT ONCE.

A. VON HOLTZ.

The fence went on past the car. A mile, a mile and a half of narrow lane, fenced in and made as nearly intruder-proof as possible.

"Wonder what I'd do," said Tommy Reames, "if another car came along from the other end?"

He deliberately tried not to think about the telegram any more. He didn't believe it. He couldn't believe it. But he couldn't ignore it, either. Nobody could: few scientists, and no human being with a normal amount of curiosity. Because the article on dominant coordinates had appeared in the *Journal of Physics* and had dealt with a state of things in which the normal coordinates of everyday existence were assumed to have changed their functions: when the coordinates of time, the vertical, the horizontal and the lateral changed places and a man went east to go up and west to go "down" and ran his street-numbers in a fourth dimension. It was mathematical foolery, from one standpoint, but it led to some fascinating if abstruse conclusions.

BUT his brain would not remain away from the subject of the telegram, even though a chicken appeared in the fenced-in lane ahead of him and went flapping wildly on before the car. It rose in mid-air, the car overtook it as it rose above the level of the hood, and there was a rolling, squawking bundle of shedding feathers tumbling over and over along the hood until it reached the slanting windshield. There it spun wildly upward, left a cloud of feather's fluttering about Tommy's head, and fell still squawking into the road behind. By the back-view mirror, Tommy could see it picking itself up and staggering dizzily back to the side of the road.

"My point was," said Tommy vexedly to himself, speaking of the article the telegram referred to, "that a man can only recognize three dimensions of space and one of time. So that if he got shot out of this cosmos altogether he wouldn't know the difference. He'd still seem to be in a three-dimensioned universe. And what is there in that stuff to get Denham in trouble?"

A house appeared ahead. A low, rambling sort of bungalow with a huge brick barn behind it. The house of Professor Denham, very certainly, and that barn was the laboratory in which he made his experiments.

Instinctively, Tommy stepped on the gas. The car leaped ahead. And then he was braking frantically. A pipe-framed gate with thinner, unpainted wire mesh filling its surface loomed before him, much too late for him to stop. There was a minor shock, a crashing and squeaking, and then a crash and shattering of glass. Tommy bent low as the top bar of the gate hit his windshield. The double glass cracked and crumpled and bent, but did not fly to bits. And the car came to a halt with its wheels intricately entangled in torn-away fence wire. The gate had been torn from its hinges and was draped rakishly over the roadster. A tire went flat with a loud hissing noise, and Tommy Reames swore softly under his breath and got out to inspect the damage.

HE was deciding that nothing irreparable was wrong when a man came bursting out of the brick building behind the house. A tall, lean, youngish man who waved his arms emphatically and approached shouting:

"You had no right to come in here! You must go away at once! You have damaged property! I will tell the Professor! You must pay for the damage! You must—"

"Damn!" said Tommy Reames. He had just seen that his radiator was punctured. A spout of ruddy, rusty water was pouring out on the grass.

The youngish man came up furiously. A pale young man, Tommy noticed. A young man with bristling, close-cropped hair and horn-rimmed spectacles before weak-looking eyes. His mouth was very full and very red, in marked contrast to the pallor of his cheeks.

"Did you not see the sign upon the gate?" he demanded angrily, in curiously stilted English. "Did you not see that trespassers are forbidden? You must go away at once! You will be prosecuted! You will be imprisoned! You—"

Tommy said irritably:

"Are you Von Holtz? My name is Reames. You telegraphed me."

The waving, lanky arms stopped in the middle of an excited gesture. The weak-looking eyes behind the lenses widened. A pink tongue licked the too-full, too-red lips.

"Reames? The Herr Reames?" Von Holtz stammered. Then he said suspiciously, "But you are not—you cannot be the Herr Reames of the article on dominant coordinates!"

"I don't know why," said Tommy annoyedly. "I'm also the Herr Reames of several other articles, such as on the mechanics of continua and the mass and inertia of the tesseract. And I believe the current *Philosophical Journal*—"

HE surveyed the spouting red stream from the radiator and shrugged ruefully.

"I wish you'd telephone the village to have somebody come out and fix my car," he said shortly, "and then tell me if this telegram is a joke or not."

He pulled out a yellow form and offered it. He had taken an instinctive dislike to the lean figure before him, but suppressed the feeling.

Von Holtz took the telegram and read it, and smoothed it out, and said agitatedly:

"But I thought the Herr Reames would be—would be a venerable gentleman! I thought—"

"You sent that wire," said Tommy. "It puzzled me just enough to make me rush out here. And I feel like a fool for having done it. What's the matter? Is it a joke?"

Von Holtz shook his head violently, even as he bit his lips.

"No! No!" he protested. "The Herr Professor Denham is in the most terrible, most deadly danger! I—I have been very nearly mad, Herr Reames. The Ragged Men may seize him!… I telegraphed to you. I have not slept for four nights. I have worked! I have racked my brains! I have gone nearly insane, trying to rescue the Herr Professor! And I—"

TOMMY stared.

"Four days?" he said. "The thing, whatever it is, has been going on for four days?"

"Five," said Von Holtz nervously. "It was only to-day that I thought of you, Herr Reames. The Herr Professor Denham had praised your articles highly. He said that you were the only man who would be able to understand his work. Five days ago—"

Tommy grunted.

"If he's been in danger for five days," he said skeptically, "he's not in such a bad fix or it'd have been over. Will you phone for a repairman? Then we'll see what it's all about."

The lean arms began to wave again as Von Holtz said desperately:

"But Herr Reames, it is urgent! The Herr Professor is in deadly danger!"

"What's the matter with him?"

"He is marooned," said Von Holtz. Again he licked his lips. "He is marooned, Herr Reames, and you alone—"

"Marooned?" said Tommy more skeptically still. "In the middle of New York State? And I alone can help him? You sound more and more as if you were playing a rather elaborate and not very funny practical joke. I've driven sixty miles to get here. What is the joke, anyhow?"

Von Holtz said despairingly:

"But it is true, Herr Reames! He is marooned. He has changed his coordinates. It was an experiment. He is marooned in the fifth dimension!"

THERE was dead silence. Tommy Reames stared blankly. Then his gorge rose. He had taken an instinctive dislike to this lean young man, anyhow.

So he stared at him, and grew very angry, and would undoubtedly have gotten into his car and turned it about and driven it away again if it had been in any shape to run. But it wasn't. One tire was flat, and the last ruddy drops from the radiator were dripping slowly on the grass. So he pulled out a cigarette case and lighted a cigarette and said sardonically:

"The fifth dimension? That seems rather extreme. Most of us get along very well with three dimensions. Four seems luxurious. Why pick on the fifth?"

Von Holtz grew pale with anger in his turn. He waved his arms, stopped, and said with stiff formality:

"If the Herr Reames will follow me into the laboratory I will show him Professor Denham and convince him of the Herr Professor's extreme danger."

Tommy had a sudden startling conviction that Von Holtz was in earnest. He might be mad, but he was in earnest. And there was undoubtedly a Professor Denham, and this was undoubtedly his home and laboratory.

"I'll look, anyway," said Tommy less skeptically. "But it is rather incredible, you know!"

"It is impossible," said Von Holtz stiffly. "You are right, Herr Reames. It is quite impossible. But it is a fact."

He turned and stalked toward the big brick barn behind the house. Tommy went with him, wholly unbelieving and yet beginning to wonder if, just possibly, there was actually an emergency of a more normal and ghastly nature in being. Von Holtz might be a madman. He might....

Gruesome, grisly thoughts ran through Tommy's head. A madman dabbling in science might do incredible things, horrible things, and then demand assistance to undo an unimaginable murder....

TOMMY was tense and alert as Von Holtz opened the door of the barnlike laboratory. He waved the lean young man on ahead.

"After you," he said curtly.

He felt almost a shiver as he entered. But the interior of the laboratory displayed no gruesome scene. It was a huge, high-ceilinged room with a concrete floor. A monster dynamo was over in one corner, coupled to a matter-of-fact four-cylinder crude-oil engine, to which was also coupled by a clutch an inexplicable windlass-drum with several hundred feet of chain wrapped around it. There were ammeters and voltmeters on a control panel, and one of the most delicate of dynamometers on its own stand, and there were work benches and a motor-driven lathe and a very complete equipment for the working of metals. And there was an electric furnace, with splashes of solidified metal on the floor beside it, and there was a miniature casting-floor, and at the farther end of the monster room there was a gigantic solenoid which evidently had once swung upon gymbals and as evidently now was broken, because it lay toppled askew upon its supports.

The only totally unidentifiable piece of apparatus in the place was one queer contrivance at one side. It looked partly like a machine-gun, because of a long brass barrel projecting from it. But the brass tube came out of a bulging casing of cast aluminum and there was no opening through which shells could be fed.

VON HOLZ moved to that contrivance, removed a cap from the end of the brass tube, looked carefully into the opening, and waved stiffly for Tommy to look in.

Again Tommy was suspicious; watched until Von Holtz was some distance away. But the instant he put his eye to the end of the brass tube he forgot all caution, all suspicion, all his doubts. He forgot everything in his amazement.

There was a lens in the end of the brass tube. It was, in fact, nothing more or less than a telescope, apparently looking at something in a closed box. But Tommy was not able to believe that he looked at an illuminated miniature for even the fraction of a second. He looked into the telescope, and he was seeing out-of-doors. Through the aluminum casting that enclosed the end of the tube. Through the thick brick walls of the laboratory. He was gazing upon a landscape such as should not—such as could not—exist upon the earth.

There were monstrous, feathery tree-ferns waving languid fronds in a breeze that came from beyond them. The telescope seemed to be pointing at a gentle slope, and those tree-ferns cut off a farther view, but there was an impenetrable tangle of breast-high foliage between the instrument and that slope, and halfway up the incline there rested a huge steel globe.

Tommy's eyes fixed themselves upon the globe. It was man-made, of course. He could see where it had been bolted together. There were glassed-in windows in its sides, and there was a door.

AS Tommy looked, that door opened partway, stopped as if someone within had hesitated, and then opened fully. A man came out. And Tommy said dazedly:

"My God!"

Because the man was a perfectly commonplace sort of individual, dressed in a perfectly commonplace fashion, and he carried a perfectly commonplace briar pipe in his hand. Moreover, Tommy recognized him. He had seen pictures of him often enough, and he was Professor Edward Denham, entitled to put practically all the letters of the alphabet after his name, the author of "Polymerization of the Pseudo-Metallic Nitrides" and the proper owner of this building and its contents. But Tommy saw him against a background of tree-ferns such as should have been extinct upon this earth since the Carboniferous Period, some millions of years ago.

He was looking hungrily at his briar pipe. Presently he began to hunt carefully about on the ground. He picked together half a handful of brownish things which had to be dried leaves. He stuffed them into the pipe, struck a match, and lighted it. He puffed away gloomily, surrounded by wholly monstrous vegetation. A butterfly fluttered over the top of the steel globe. Its wings were fully a yard across. It flittered lightly to a plant and seemed to wait, and abruptly a vivid carmine blossom opened wide; wide enough to admit it.

Denham watched curiously enough, smoking the rank and plainly unsatisfying dried leaves. He turned his head and spoke over his shoulder. The door opened again. Again Tommy Reames was dazed. Because a girl came out of the huge steel sphere—and she was a girl of the most modern and most normal sort. A trim sport frock, slim silken legs, bobbed hair....

Tommy did not see her face until she turned, smiling, to make some comment to Denham. Then he saw that she was breath-takingly pretty. He swore softly under his breath.

THE butterfly backed clumsily out of the gigantic flower. It flew lightly away, its many-colored wings brilliant in the sunshine. And the huge crimson blossom closed slowly.

Denham watched the butterfly go away. His eyes returned to the girl who was smiling at the flying thing, now out of the field of vision of the telescope. And there was utter discouragement visible in every line of Denham's figure. Tommy saw the girl suddenly reach out her hand and put it on Denham's shoulder. She patted it, speaking in an evident attempt to encourage him. She smiled, and talked coaxingly, and presently Denham made a queer, arrested gesture and went heavily back into the steel globe. She followed him, though she looked wearily all about before the door closed behind her, and when Denham could not see her face, her expression was tired and anxious indeed.

Tommy had forgotten Von Holtz, had forgotten the laboratory, had forgotten absolutely everything. If his original suspicions of Von Holtz had been justified, he could have been killed half a dozen times over. He was oblivious to everything but the sight before his eyes.

Now he felt a touch on his shoulder and drew his head away with a jerk. Von Holtz was looking down at him, very pale, with his weak-looking eyes anxious.

"They are still all right?" he demanded.

"Yes," said Tommy dazedly. "Surely. Who is that girl?"

"That is the Herr Professor's daughter Evelyn," said Von Holtz uneasily. "I suggest, Herr Reames, that you swing the dimensoscope about."

"The—what?" asked Tommy, still dazed by what he had seen.

"The dimensoscope. This." Von Holtz shifted the brass tube. The whole thing was mounted so that it could be swung in any direction. The mounting was exactly like that of a normal telescope. Tommy instantly put his eye to the eyepiece again.

HE saw more tree-ferns, practically the duplicates of the background beyond the globe. Nothing moved save small, fugitive creatures among their fronds. He swung the telescope still farther. The landscape swept by before his eyes. The tree-fern forest drew back. He saw the beginning of a vast and noisome morass, over which lay a thick haze as of a stream raised by the sun. He saw something move in that morass; something huge and horrible with a long and snake-like neck and the tiniest of heads at the end of it. But he could not see the thing clearly.

He swung the telescope yet again. And he looked over miles and miles of level, haze-blanketed marsh. Here and there were clumps of taller vegetation. Here and there were steaming, desolate pools. And three or four times he saw monstrous objects moving about clumsily in the marsh-land.

But then a glitter at the skyline caught his eye. He tilted the telescope to see more clearly, and suddenly he caught his breath. There, far away at the very horizon, was a city. It was tall and gleaming and very strange. No earthly city ever flung its towers so splendidly high and soaring. No city ever built by man gave off the fiery gleam of gold from all its walls and pinnacles. It looked like an artist's dream, hammered out in precious metal, with its outlines softened by the haze of distance.

And something was moving in the air near the city. Staring, tense, again incredulous, Tommy Reames strained his eyes and saw that it was a machine. An air-craft; a flying-machine of a type wholly unlike anything ever built upon the planet Earth. It swept steadily and swiftly toward the city, dwindling as it went. It swooped downward toward one of the mighty spires of the city of golden gleams, and vanished.

IT was with a sense of shock, of almost physical shock, that Tommy came back to realization of his surroundings to feel Von Holtz's hand upon his shoulder and to hear the lean young man saying harshly:

"Well, Herr Reames? Are you convinced that I did not lie to you? Are you convinced that the Herr Professor Denham is in need of help?"

Tommy blinked dazedly as he looked around the laboratory again. Brick walls, an oil-spattered crude-oil engine in one corner, a concrete floor and an electric furnace and a casting-box....

"Why—yes...." said Tommy dazedly. "Yes. Of course!" Clarity came to his brain with a jerk. He did not understand at all, but he believed what he had seen. Denham and his daughter were somewhere in some other dimension, yet within range of the extraordinary device he had looked through. And they were in trouble. So much was evident from their poses and their manner. "Of course," he repeated. "They're—there, wherever it is, and they can't get back. They don't seem to be in any imminent danger...."

Von Holtz licked his lips.

"The Ragged Men have not found them yet," he said in a hushed, harsh voice. "Before they went in the globe we saw the Ragged Men. We watched them. If they do find the Herr Professor and his daughter, they will kill them very slowly, so that they will take days of screaming agony to die. It is that that I am afraid of, Herr Reames. The Ragged Men roam the tree-fern forests. If they find the Herr Professor they will trace each nerve to its root of agony until he dies. And we will be able only to watch...."

CHAPTER II

"THE thing is," said Tommy feverishly, "that we've got to find a way to get them back. Whether it duplicates Denham's results or not. How far away are they?"

"A few hundred yards, perhaps," said Von Holtz wearily, "or ten million miles. It is the same thing. They are in a place where the fifth dimension is the dominant coordinate."

Tommy was pacing up and down the laboratory. He stopped and looked through the eyepiece of the extraordinary vision apparatus. He tore himself away from it again.

"How does this thing work?" he demanded.

Von Holtz began to unscrew two wing-nuts which kept the top of the aluminum casting in place.

"It is the first piece of apparatus which Professor Denham made," he said precisely. "I know the theory, but I cannot duplicate it. Every dimension is at right angles to all other dimensions, of course. The Herr Professor has a note, here—"

He stopped his unscrewing to run over a heap of papers on the workbench—papers over which he seemed to have been poring desperately at the time of Tommy's arrival. He handed a sheet to Tommy, who read:

"If a creature who was aware of only two dimensions made two right-angled objects and so placed them that all the angles formed by the combination were right angles, he would contrive a figure represented by the corner of a box; he would discover a third dimension. Similarly, if a three-dimensioned man took three right angles and placed them so that all the angles formed were right angles, he would discover a fourth dimension. This, however, would probably be the time dimension, and to travel in time would instantly be fatal. But with four right angles he could discover a fifth dimension, and with five right angles he could discover a sixth...."

TOMMY REAMES put down the paper impatiently.

"Of course" he said brusquely. "I know all that stuff. But up to the present time nobody has been able to put together even three right angles, in practise."

Von Holtz had returned to the unscrewing of the wing-nuts. He lifted off the cover of the dimensoscope.

"It is the thing the Herr Professor did not confide to me," he said bitterly. "The secret. The one secret! Look in here."

Tommy looked. The objective-glass at the end of the telescope faced a mirror, which was inclined to its face at an angle of forty-five degrees. A beam of light from the objective would be reflected to a second mirror, twisted in a fashion curiously askew. Then the light would go to a third mirror....

Tommy looked at that third mirror, and instantly his eyes ached. He closed them and opened them again. Again they stung horribly. It was exactly the sort of eye-strain which comes of looking through a lens which does not focus exactly, or through a strange pair of eyeglasses. He could see the third mirror, but his eyes hurt the instant they looked upon it, as if that third mirror were distorted in an impossible fashion. He was forced to draw them away. He could see, though, that somehow that third mirror would reflect his imaginary beam of light into a fourth mirror of which he could see only the edge. He moved his head—and still saw only the edge of a mirror. He was sure of what he saw, because he could look into the wavy, bluish translucency all glass shows upon its edge. He could even see the thin layer of silver backing. But he could not put himself into a position in which more than the edge of that mirror was visible.

"Good Lord!" said Tommy Reames feverishly. "That mirror—"

"A mirror at forty-five degrees," said Von Holtz precisely, "reflects light at a right angle. There are four mirrors, and each bends a ray of light through a right angle which is also a right angle to all the others. The result is that the dimensoscope looks into what is a fifth dimension, into which no man ever looked before. But I cannot move other mirrors into the positions they have in this instrument. I do not know how."

TOMMY shook his head impatiently, staring at the so-simple, yet incredible device whose theory had been mathematically proven numberless times, but never put into practice before.

"Having made this device," said Von Holtz, "the Herr Professor constructed what he termed a catapult. It was a coil of wire, like the large machine there. It jerked a steel ball first vertically, then horizontally, then laterally, then in a fourth-dimensional direction, and finally projected it violently off in a fifth-dimensional path. He made small hollow steel balls and sent a butterfly, a small sparrow, and finally a cat into that other world. The steel balls opened of themselves and freed those creatures. They seemed to suffer no distress. Therefore he concluded that it would be safe for him to go, himself. His daughter refused to permit him to go alone, and he was so sure of his safety that he allowed her to enter the globe with him. She did. I worked the catapult which flung the globe in the fifth dimension, and his device for returning failed to operate. Hence he is marooned."

"But the big catapult—"

"Can you not see that the big catapult is broken?" demanded Von Holtz bitterly. "A special metal is required for the missing parts. That, I know how to make. Yes. I can supply that. But I cannot shape it! I cannot design the gears which will move it as it should be moved! I cannot make another dimensoscope. I cannot, Herr Reames, calculate any method of causing four right angles to be all at right angles to each other. It is my impossibility! It is for that that I have appealed to you. You see it has been done. I see that it is done. I can make the metal which alone can be moved in the necessary direction. But I cannot calculate any method of moving it in that direction!

If you can do so, Herr Reames, we can perhaps save the Herr Professor Denham. If you cannot—Gott! The death he will die is horrible to think of!"

"And his daughter," said Tommy grimly. "His daughter, also."

HE paced up and down the laboratory again. Von Holtz moved to the workbench from which he had taken Denham's note. There was a pile of such memoranda, thumbed over and over. And there were papers in the angular, precise handwriting which was Von Holtz's own, and calculations and speculations and the remains of frantic efforts to work out, somehow, the secret which as one manifestation had placed one mirror so that it hurt the eyes to look at it, and one other mirror so that from every angle of a normal existence, one could see only the edge.

"I have worked, Herr Reames," said Von Holtz drearily. "Gott! How I have worked! But the Herr Professor kept some things secret, and that so-essential thing is one of them."

Presently he said tiredly:

"The dimension-traveling globe was built in this laboratory. It rested here." He pointed. "The Herr Professor was laughing and excited at the moment of departure. His daughter smiled at me through the window of the globe. There was an under-carriage with wheels upon it. You cannot see those wheels through the dimensoscope. They got into the globe and closed the door. The Herr Professor nodded to me through the glass window. The dynamo was running at its fullest speed. The laboratory smelled of hot oil, and of ozone from the sparks. I lifted my hand, and the Herr Professor nodded again, and I threw the switch. This switch, Herr Reames! It sparked as I closed it, and the flash partly blinded me. But I saw the globe rush toward the giant catapult yonder. It leaped upward into the huge coil, which whirled madly. Dazed, I saw the globe hanging suspended in mid-air, two feet from the floor. It shook! Once! Twice! With violence! Suddenly its outline became hazy and distorted. My eyes ached with looking at it. And then it was gone!"

VON HOLTZ'S arms waved melodramatically.

"I rushed to the dimensoscope and gazed through it into the fifth dimension. I saw the globe floating onward through the air, toward that bank of glossy ferns. I saw it settle and turn over, and then slowly right itself as it came to rest. The Herr Professor got out of it. I saw him through the instrument which could look into the dimension into which he had gone. He waved his hand to me. His daughter joined him, surveying the strange cosmos in which they were. The Herr Professor plucked some of the glossy ferns, took photographs, then got back into the globe.

"I awaited its return to our own world. I saw it rock slightly as he worked upon the apparatus within. I knew that when it vanished from the dimensoscope it would have returned to our own universe. But it remained as before. It did not move. After three hours of anguished waiting, the Herr Professor came out and made signals to me of despair. By gestures, because no sound could come through the dimensoscope itself, he begged me to assist him. And I was helpless! Made helpless by the Herr Professor's own secrecy! For four days and nights I have toiled, hoping desperately to discover what the Herr Professor had hidden from me. At last I thought of you. I telegraphed to you. If you can assist me...."

"I'm going to try it, of course," said Tommy shortly.

He paced back and forth. He stopped and looked through the brass-tubed telescope. Giant tree-ferns, unbelievable but real. The steel globe resting partly overturned upon a bank of glossy ferns. Breast-high, incredible foliage between the point of vision and that extraordinary vehicle.

WHILE Tommy had been talking and listening, while he had been away from the eyepiece, one or other of the occupants of the globe had emerged from it. The door was open. But now the girl came bounding suddenly through the ferns. She called, though it seemed to Tommy that there was a curious air of caution even in her calling. She was excited, hopefully excited.

Denham came out of the globe with a clumsy club in his hand. But Evelyn caught his arm and pointed up into the sky. Denham stared, and then began to make wild and desperate gestures as if trying to attract attention to himself.

Tommy watched for minutes, and then swung the dimensoscope around. It was extraordinary, to be sitting in the perfectly normal brick-walled laboratory, looking into a slender brass tube, and seeing another universe entirely, another wild and unbelievable landscape.

The tree-fern forest drew back and the vast and steaming morass was again in view. There were distant bright golden gleams from the city. But Tommy was searching the sky, looking in the sky of a world in the fifth dimension for a thing which would make a man gesticulate hopefully.

He found it. It was an aircraft, startlingly close through the telescope. A single figure was seated at its controls, motionless as if bored, with exactly the air of a weary truck driver piloting a vehicle along a roadway he does not really see. And Tommy, being near enough to see the pilot's pose, could see the aircraft clearly. It was totally unlike a terrestrial airplane. A single huge and thick wing supported it. But the wing was angular and clumsy-seeming, and its form was devoid of the grace of an earthly aircraft wing, and there was no tail whatever to give it the appearance of a living thing. There was merely a long, rectangular wing with a framework beneath it, and a shimmering thing which was certainly not a screw propeller, but which seemed to draw it.

IT moved on steadily and swiftly, dwindling in the distance, with its motionless pilot seated before a mass of corded bundles. It looked as if this were a freight plane of some sort, and therefore made in a strictly utilitarian fashion.

It vanished in the haze above the monster swamp, going in a straight line for the golden city at the world's edge.

Tommy stared at it, long after it had ceased to be visible. Then he saw a queer movement on the earth near the edge of the morass. Figures were moving. Human figures. He saw four of them, shaking clenched fists and capering insanely, seeming to bellow insults after the oblivious and now invisible flying thing. He could see that they were nearly naked, and that one of them carried a spear. But the indubitable glint of metal was reflected from one of them for an instant, when some metal accoutrement about him glittered in the sunlight.

They moved from sight behind thick, feathery foliage, and Tommy swung back the brass tube to see the globe again. Denham and his daughter were staring in the direction in which Tommy had seen those human figures. Denham clutched his clumsy club grimly. His face was drawn and his figure tensed. And suddenly Evelyn spoke quietly, and the two of then dived into the fern forest and disappeared. Minutes later they returned, dragging masses of tree-fern fronds with which they masked the globe from view. They worked hastily, desperately, concealing the steel vehicle from sight. And then Denham stared tensely all about, shading his eyes with his hand. He and the girl withdrew cautiously into the forest.

IT was minutes later that Tommy was roused by Von Holtz's hand on his shoulder.

"What has happened, Herr Reames?" he asked uneasily. "The—Ragged Men?"

"I saw men," said Tommy briefly, "shaking clenched fists at an aircraft flying overhead. And Denham and his daughter have hidden the globe behind a screen of foliage."

Von Holtz licked his lips fascinatedly.

"The Ragged Men," he said in a hushed voice. "The Herr Professor called them that, because they cannot be of the people who live in the Golden City.

They hate the people of the Golden City. I think that they are bandits; renegades, perhaps. They live in the tree-fern forests and scream curses at the airships which fly overhead. And they are afraid of those airships."

"How long did Denham use this thing to look through, before he built his globe?"

Von Holtz considered.

"Immediately it worked," he said at last, "he began work on a small catapult. It took him one week to devise exactly how to make that. He experimented with it for some days and began to make the large globe. That took nearly two months—the globe and the large catapult together. And also the dimensoscope was at hand. His daughter looked through it more than he did, or myself."

"He should have known what he was up against," said Tommy, frowning. "He ought to have taken guns, at least. Is he armed?"

Von Holtz shook his head.

"He expected to return at once," he said desperately. "Do you see, Herr Reames, the position it puts me in? I may be suspected of murder! I am the Herr Professor's assistant. He disappears. Will I not be accused of having put him out of the way?"

"No," said Tommy thoughtfully. "You won't." He glanced through the brass tube and paced up and down the room. "You telephone for someone to repair my car," he said suddenly and abruptly. "I am going to stay here and work this thing out. I've got just the glimmering of an idea. But I'll need my car in running order, in case we have to go out and get materials in a hurry."

VON HOLTZ bowed stiffly and went out of the laboratory. Tommy looked after him. Even moved to make sure he was gone. And then Tommy Reames went quickly to the work bench on which were the littered notes and calculations Von Holtz had been using and which were now at his disposal. But Tommy did not leaf through them. He reached under the blotter beneath the whole pile. He had seen Von Holtz furtively push something out of sight, and he had disliked and distrusted Von Holtz from the beginning. Moreover, it was pretty thoroughly clear that Denham had not trusted him too much. A trusted assistant should be able to understand, at least, any experiment performed in a laboratory.

A folded sheet of paper came out. Tommy glanced at it.

"You messed things up right! Denham marooned and you got nothing. No plans or figures either. When you get them, you get your money. If you don't you are out of luck. If this Reames guy can't fix up what you want it'll be just too bad for you."

There was no salutation nor any signature beyond a scrawled and sprawling "J."

Tommy Reames' jaw set grimly. He folded the scrap of paper and thrust it back out of sight again.

"Pretty!" he said harshly. "So a gentleman named 'J' is going to pay Von Holtz for plans or calculations it is hoped I'll provide! Which suggests—many things! But at least I'll have Von Holtz's help until he thinks my plans or calculations are complete. So that's all right...."

Tommy could not be expected, of course, to guess that the note he had read was quite astounding proof of the interest taken in non-Euclidean geometry by a vice king of Chicago, or that the ranking beer baron of that metropolis was the man who was so absorbed in abstruse theoretic physics.

TOMMY moved toward the great solenoid which lay askew upon its wrecked support. It had drawn the steel globe toward it, had made that globe vibrate madly, twice, and then go hazy and vanish. It had jerked the globe in each of five directions, each at right angles to all the others, and had released it when started in the fifth dimension. The huge coil was quite nine feet across and would take the steel globe easily. It was pivoted in concentric rings which made up a set of gymbals far more elaborate than were ever used to suspend a mariner's compass aboard ship.

There were three rings, one inside the other. And two rings will take care of any motion in three dimensions. These rings were pivoted, too, so that an unbelievably intricate series of motions could be given to the solenoid within them all. But the device was broken, now. A pivot had given away, and shaft and socket alike had vanished. Tommy became absorbed. Some oddity bothered him....

He pieced the thing together mentally. And he exclaimed suddenly. There had been four rings of metal! One was gone! He comprehended, very suddenly. The third mirror in the dimensoscope was the one so strangely distorted by its position, which was at half of a right angle to all the dimensions of human experience. It was the third ring in the solenoid's supports which had vanished. And Tommy, staring at the gigantic apparatus and summoning all his theoretic knowledge and all his brain to work, saw the connection between the two things.

"The time dimension and the world-line," he said sharply, excited in spite of himself. "Revolving in the time dimension means telescoping in the world-line…. It would be a strain no matter could endure…."

THE mirror in the dimensoscope was not pointing in a fourth dimension. It did not need to. It was reflecting light at a right angle, and hence needed to be only at half of a right angle to the two courses of the beam it reflected. But to whirl the steel globe into a fifth dimension, the solenoid's support had for one instant to revolve in time! For the fraction of a second it would have literally to pass through its own substance. It would be required to undergo precisely the sort of strain involved in turning a hollow seamless metal globe, inside out! No metal could stand such a strain. No form of matter known to man could endure it.

"It would explode!" said Tommy excitedly to himself, alone in the great bare laboratory. "Steel itself would vaporize! It would wreck the place!"

And then he looked blank. Because the place had very obviously not been wrecked. And yet a metal ring had vanished, leaving no trace….

Von Holtz came back. He looked frightened.

"A—a repairman, Herr Reames," he said, stammering, "is on the way. And—Herr Reames…."

Tommy barely heard him. For a moment, Tommy was all scientist, confronted with the inexplicable, yet groping with a blind certainty toward a conclusion he very vaguely foresaw. He waved his hand impatiently….

"The Herr Jacaro is on the way here," stammered Von Holtz.

TOMMY blinked, remembering that Von Holtz had told him he could make a certain metal, the only metal which could be moved in the fourth dimension.

"Jacaro?" he said blankly.

"The—friend of the Herr Professor Denham. He advanced the money for the Herr Professor's experiments."

Tommy heard him with only half his brain, though that half instantly decided that Von Holtz was lying. The only Jacaro Tommy knew of was a prominent gangster from Chicago, who had recently cemented his position in Chicago's underworld by engineering the amalgamation of two once-rival gangs.

Tommy knew, in a vague fashion, that Von Holtz was frightened. That he was terrified in some way. And that he was inordinately suspicious of someone, and filled with a queer desperation.

"Well?" said Tommy abstractedly. The thought he needed was coming. A metal which would have full tensile strength up to a certain instant, and then disrupt itself without violence into a gas, a vapor…. It would be an alloy, perhaps. It would be….

He struck at his own head with his clenched fist, angrily demanding that his brain bring forth the thought that was forming slowly. The metal that could be revolved in time without producing a disastrous explosion and without requiring an impossible amount of power….

HE did not see Von Holtz looking in the eyepiece of the dimensoscope. He stared at nothing, thinking concentratedly, putting every bit of energy into sheer thought. And suddenly, like the explosion he sought a way to avoid, the answer came, blindingly clear.

He surveyed that answer warily. A tremendous excitement filled him.

"I've got it!" he said softly to himself. "By God, I know how he did the thing!"

And as if through a mist the figure of Von Holtz became clear before his eyes. Von Holtz was looking into the dimensoscope tube. He was staring into that other, extraordinary world in which Denham and his daughter were marooned. And Von Holtz's face was utterly, deathly white, and he was making frantic, repressed gestures, and whispering little whimpering phrases to himself. They were unintelligible, but the deathly pallor of his cheeks, and the fascinated, dribbling fullness of his lips brought Tommy Reames suddenly down to earth.

"What's happening?" demanded Tommy sharply.

Von Holtz did not answer. He made disjointed, moaning little exclamations to himself. He was twitching horribly as he looked through the telescope into that other world….

Tommy flung him aside and clapped his own eye to the eyepiece. And then he groaned.

THE telescope was pointed at the steel globe upon that ferny bank, no more than a few hundred yards away but two dimensions removed from Earth. The screening mass of tree-fronds had been torn away. A swarm of ragged, half-naked men was gathered about the globe. They were armed with spears and clubs, in the main, but there were other weapons of intricate design whose uses Tommy could not even guess at. He did not try. He was watching the men as they swarmed about and over the steel sphere. Their faces were brutal and savage, and now they were distorted with an insane hate. It was the same awful, gibbering hatred he had sensed in the caperings of the four he had seen bellowing vituperation at an airplane.

They were not savages. Somehow he could not envision them as primitive. Their features were hard-bitten, seamed with hatred and with vice unspeakable. And they were white. The instant impression any man would have received was that here were broken men; fugitives, bandits, assassins. Here were renegades or worse from some higher, civilized race.

They battered hysterically upon the steel globe. It was not the attack of savages upon a strange thing. It was the assault of desperate, broken men upon a thing they hated. A glass pane splintered and crashed. Spears were thrust into the opening, while mouths opened as if in screams of insane fury. And then, suddenly, the door of the globe flew wide.

The Ragged Men did not wait for anyone to come out. They fought each other to get into the opening, their eyes glaring madly, filled with the lust to kill.

CHAPTER III

A BATTERED and antiquated flivver came chugging down the wire-fenced lane to the laboratory, an hour later. It made a prodigious din, and Tommy Reames went out to meet it. He was still a little pale. He had watched the steel globe turned practically inside out by the Ragged Men. He had seen them bringing out cameras, cushions, and even the padding of the walls, to be torn to bits in a truly maniacal fury. But he had not seen one sign of a human being killed. Denham and his daughter had not been in the globe when it was found and ransacked. So far, then, they were probably safe. Tommy had seen them vanish into the tree-fern forest. They had been afraid, and with good reason. What dangers they might encounter in the fern forest he could not guess. How long they would escape the search of the Ragged Men, he could not know. How he could ever hope to find them if he succeeded in duplicating Denham's dimension-traveling apparatus he could not even think of, just now. But the Ragged Men were not searching the fern forest. So much was sure. They were encamped by the steel sphere, and a scurvy-looking lot they were.

Coming out of the brick laboratory, Tommy saw a brawny figure getting out of the antiquated flivver whose arrival had been so thunderous. That brawny figure nodded to him and grinned. Tommy recognized him. The red-headed, broad-shouldered filling station attendant in the last village, who had given him specific directions for reaching this place.

"You hit that gate a lick, didn't you?" asked the erstwhile filling station attendant amiably. "Mr. Von Holtz said you had a flat and a busted radiator. That right?"

TOMMY nodded. The red-headed man walked around the car, scratched his chin, and drew out certain assorted tools. He put them on the grass with great precision, pumped a gasoline blow-torch to pressure and touched a match to its priming-basin, and while the gasoline flamed smokily he made a half dozen casual movements with a file, and the broken radiator tube was exposed for repair.

He went back to the torch and observed placidly:

"The Professor ain't around, is he?"

Tommy shook his head.

"Thought not," said the red-headed one. "He gen'rally comes out and talks a while. I helped him build some of them dinkuses in the barn yonder."

Tommy said eagerly:

"Say, which of those things did you help him build? That big thing with the solenoid—the coil?"

"Yeah. How'd it work?" The red-headed one set a soldering iron in place and began to jack up the rear wheel to get at the tire. "Crazy idea, if you ask me. I told Miss Evelyn so. She laughed and said she'd be in the ball when it was tried. Did it work?"

"Too damn well," said Tommy briefly. "I've got to repair that solenoid. How about a job helping?"

The red-headed man unfastened the lugs of the rim, kicked the tire speculatively, and said, "Gone to hell." He put on the spare tire with ease and dispatch.

"Um," he said. "How about that Mr. Von Holtz? Is he goin' to boss the job?"

"He is not," said Tommy, with a shade of grimness in his tone.

THE red-headed man nodded and took the soldering iron in hand. He unwound a strip of wire solder, mended the radiator tube with placid ease, and seemed to bang the cooling-flanges with a total lack of care. They went magically back into place, and it took close inspection to see that the radiator had been damaged.

"She's all right," he observed. He regarded Tommy impersonally. "Suppose you tell me how come you horn in on this," he suggested, "an' maybe I'll play. That guy Von Holtz is a crook, if you ask me about him."

Tommy ran his hand across his forehead, and told him.

"Um," said the red-headed man calmly. "I think I'll go break Mr. Von Holtz's neck. I got me a hunch."

He took two deliberate steps forward. But Tommy said:

"I saw Denham not an hour ago. So far, he's all right. How long he'll be all right is a question. But I'm going after him."

The red-headed man scrutinized him exhaustively.

"Um. I might try that myself. I kinda like the Professor. An' Miss Evelyn. My name's Smithers. Let's go look through the dinkus the Professor made."

They went together into the laboratory. Von Holtz was looking through the dimensoscope. He started back as they entered, and looked acutely uneasy when he saw the red-headed man.

"How do you do," he said nervously. "They—the Ragged Men—have just brought in a dead man. But it is not the Herr Professor."

Without a word, Tommy took the brass tube in his hand. Von Holtz moved away, biting his lips. Tommy stared into that strange other world.

THE steel sphere lay as before, slightly askew upon a bank of glossy ferns. But its glass windows were shattered, and fragments of everything it had contained were scattered about. The Ragged Men had made a camp and built a fire. Some of them were roasting meat—the huge limb of a monstrous animal with a scaly, reptilian hide. Others were engaged in vehement argument over the body of one of their number, lying sprawled out upon the ground.

Tommy spoke without moving his eyes from the eyepiece.

"I saw Denham with a club just now. This man was killed by a club."

The Ragged Men in the other world debated acrimoniously. One of them pointed to the dead man's belt, and spread out his hands. Something was missing from the body. Tommy saw, now, three or four other men with objects that looked rather like policemen's truncheons, save that they were made of glittering metal. They were plainly weapons. Denham, then, was armed—if he could understand how the weapon was used.

The Ragged Men debated, and presently their dispute attracted the attention of a man with a huge black beard. He rose from where he sat gnawing at a piece of meat and moved grandly toward the disputatious group. They parted at his approach, but a single member continued the debate against even the bearded giant. The bearded one plucked the glittering truncheon from his belt. The disputatious one gasped in fear and flung himself desperately forward. But the bearded man kept the truncheon pointed steadily.... The man who assailed him staggered, reached close enough to strike a single blow, and collapsed. The bearded man pointed the metal truncheon at him as he lay upon the ground. He heaved convulsively, and was still.

The bearded man went back to his seat and picked up the gnawed bit of meat again. The dispute had ceased. The chattering group of men dispersed.

TOMMY was about to leave the eyepiece of the instrument when a movement nearby caught his eye. A head peered cautiously toward the encampment. A second rose beside it. Denham and his daughter Evelyn. They were apparently no more than thirty feet from the dimensoscope. Tommy could see them talking cautiously, saw Denham lift and examine a metal truncheon like the bearded man's, and force his daughter to accept it. He clutched a club, himself, with a grim satisfaction.

Moments later they vanished quietly in the thick fern foliage, and though Tommy swung the dimensoscope around in every direction, he could see nothing of their retreat.

He rose from that instrument with something approaching hopefulness. He'd seen Evelyn very near and very closely. She did not look happy, but she did look alert rather than worn. And Denham was displaying a form of competence in the face of danger which was really more than would have been expected in a Ph.D., a M.A., and other academic distinctions running to most of the letters of the alphabet.

"I've just seen Denham and Evelyn again," said Tommy crisply. "They're safe so far. And I've seen one of the weapons of the Ragged Men in use. If we can get a couple of automatics and some cartridges to Denham, he'll be safe until we can repair the big solenoid."

"There was the small catapult," said Von Holtz bitterly, "but it was dismantled. The Herr Professor saw me examining it, and he dismantled it. So that I did not learn how to calculate the way of changing the position—"

TOMMY'S eyes rested queerly on Von Holtz for a moment.

"You know how to make the metal required," he said suddenly. "You'd better get busy making it. Plenty of it. We'll need it."

Von Holtz stared at him, his weak eyes almost frightened.

"You *know*? You know how to combine the right angles?"

"I think so," said Tommy. "I've got to find out if I'm right. Will you make the metal?"

Von Holtz bit at his too-red lips.

"But Herr Reames!" he said stridently, "I wish to know the equation! Tell me the method of pointing a body in a fourth or a fifth direction. It is only fair—"

"Denham didn't tell you," said Tommy.

Von Holtz's arms jerked wildly.

"But I will not make the metal! I insist upon being told the equation! I insist upon it! I will not make the metal if you do not tell me!"

Smithers was in the laboratory, of course. He had been surveying the big solenoid-catapult and scratching his chin reflectively. Now he turned.

BUT Tommy took Von Holtz by the shoulders. And Tommy's hands were the firm and sinewy hands of a sportsman, if his brain did happen to be the brain of a scientist. Von Holtz writhed in his grip.

"There is only one substance which could be the metal I need, Von Holtz," he said gently. "Only one substance is nearly three-dimensional. Metallic ammonium! It's known to exist, because it makes a mercury amalgam, but nobody has been able to isolate it because nobody has been able to give it a fourth dimension—duration in time. Denham did it. You can do it. And I need it, and you'd better set to work at the job. You'll be very sorry if you don't, Von Holtz!"

Smithers said with a vast calmness.

"I got me a hunch. So if y'want his neck broke...."

Tommy released Von Holtz and the lean young man gasped and sputtered and gesticulated wildly in a frenzy of rage.

"He'll make it," said Tommy coldly. "Because he doesn't dare not to!"

Von Holtz went out of the laboratory, his weak-looking eyes staring and wild, and his mouth working.

"He'll be back," said Tommy briefly. "You've got to make a small model of that big catapult, Smithers. Can you do it?"

"Sure," said Smithers. "The ring'll be copper tubing, with pin-bearings. Wind a coil on the lathe. It'll be kinda rough, but it'll do. But gears, now...."

"I'll attend to them. You know how to work that metallic ammonium?"

"If that's what it was," agreed Smithers. "I worked it for the Professor."

Tommy leaned close and whispered:

"You never made any gears of that. But did you make some springs?"

"Uh-huh!"

Tommy grinned joyously.

"Then we're set and I'm right! Von Holtz wants a mathematical formula, and no one on earth could write one, but we don't need it!"

SMITHERS rummaged around the laboratory with a casual air, acquired this and that and the other thing, and set to work with an astounding absence of waste motions. From time to time he inspected the great catapult thoughtfully, verified some impression, and went about the construction of another part.

And when Von Holtz did not return, Tommy hunted for him. He suddenly remembered hearing his car motor start. He found his car missing. He swore, then, and grimly began to hunt for a telephone in the house. But before he had raised central he heard the deep-toned purring of the motor again. His car was coming swiftly back to the house. And he saw, through a window, that Von Holtz was driving it.

The lean young man got out of it, his face white with passion. He started for the laboratory. Tommy intercepted him.

"I—went to get materials for making the metal," said Von Holtz hoarsely, repressing his rage with a great effort. "I shall begin at once, Herr Reames."

Tommy said nothing whatever. Von Holtz was lying. Of course. He carried nothing in the way of materials. But he had gone away from the house, and Tommy knew as definitely as if Von Holtz had told him, that Von Holtz had gone off to communicate in safety with someone who signed his correspondence with a J.

Von Holtz went into the laboratory. The four-cylinder motor began to throb at once. The whine of the dynamo arose almost immediately after. Von Holtz came out of the laboratory and dived into a shed that adjoined the brick building. He remained in there.

Tommy looked at the trip register on his speedometer. Like most people with methodical minds, he had noted the reading on arriving at a new destination. Now he knew how far Von Holtz had gone. He had been to the village and back.

"Meaning," said Tommy grimly to himself, "that the J who wants plans and calculations is either in the village or at the end of a long-distance wire. And Von Holtz said he was on the way. He'll probably turn up and try to bribe me."

HE went back into the laboratory and put his eye to the eyepiece of the dimensoscope. Smithers had his blow-torch going and was busily accumulating an apparently unrelated series of discordant bits of queerly-shaped metal. Tommy looked through at the strange mad world he could see through the eyepiece.

The tree-fern forest was still. The encampment of the Ragged Men was nearly quiet. Sunset seemed to be approaching in this other world, though it was still bright outside the laboratory. The hours of day and night were obviously not the same in the two worlds, so close together that a man could be flung from one to the other by a mechanical contrivance.

The sun seemed larger, too, than the orb which lights our normal earth. When Tommy swung the vision instrument about to search for it, he found a great red ball quite four times the diameter of our own sun, neatly bisected by the horizon. Tommy watched, waiting for it to sink. But it did not sink straight downward as the sun seems to do in all temperate latitudes. It descended, yes, but it moved along the horizon as it sank. Instead of a direct and forthright dip downward, the sun seemed to progress along the horizon, dipping more deeply as it swam. And Tommy watched it blankly.

"It's not our sun.... But it's not our world. Yet it revolves, and there are men on it. And a sun that size would bake the earth.... And it's sinking at an angle that would only come at a latitude of—"

That was the clue. He understood at once. The instrument through which he regarded the strange world looked out upon the polar regions of that world. Here, where the sun descended slantwise, were the high latitudes, the coldest spaces upon all the whole planet. And if here there were the gigantic growths of a carboniferous era, the tropic regions of this planet must be literal infernos.

And then he saw in its gradual descent the monster sun was going along behind the golden city, and the outlines of its buildings, the magnificence of its spires, were limned clearly for him against the dully glowing disk.

Nowhere upon earth had such a city ever been dreamed of. No man had ever envisioned such a place, where far-flung arches interconnected soaring, towering columns, where curves of perfect grace were united in forms of utterly perfect proportion....

THE sunlight died, and dusk began and deepened, and vividly brilliant stars began to come out overhead, and Tommy suddenly searched the heavens eagerly for familiar constellations. And found not one. All the stars were strange. These stars seemed larger and much more near than the tiny pinpoints that blink down upon our earth.

And then he swung the instrument again and saw great fires roaring and the Ragged Men crouched about them. Within them, rather, because they had built fires about themselves as if to make a wall of flame. And once Tommy saw twin, monstrous eyes, gazing from the blackness of the tree-fern forest. They were huge eyes, and they were far apart, so that the head of the creature who used them must have been enormous. And they were all of fifteen feet above the ground when they speculatively looked over the ring of fires and the ragged, degraded men within them. Then that creature, whatever it was, turned away and vanished.

But Tommy felt a curious shivering horror of the thing. It had moved soundlessly, without a doubt, because not one of the Ragged Men had noted its presence. It had been kept away by the fires. But Denham and Evelyn were somewhere in the tree-fern forest, and they would not dare to make fires....

Tommy drew away from the dimensoscope, shivering. He had been looking only, but the place into which he looked was real, and the dangers that lay hidden there were very genuine, and there was a man and a girl of his own race and time struggling desperately, without arms or hope, to survive.

SMITHERS was casually fitting together an intricate array of little rings made of copper tubing. There were three of them, and each was fitted into the next largest by pins which enabled them to spin noiselessly and swiftly at the touch of Smithers' finger. He had them spinning now, each in a separate direction, and the effect was bewildering.

As Tommy watched, Smithers stopped them, oiled the pins carefully, and painstakingly inserted a fourth ring. Only this ring was of a white metal that looked somehow more pallid than silver. It had a whiteness like that of ivory beneath its metallic gleam.

Tommy blinked.

"Did Von Holtz give you that metal?" he asked suddenly.

Smithers looked up and puffed at a short brown pipe.

"Nope. There was some splashes of it by the castin' box. I melted 'em together an' run a ring. Pressed it to shape; y' can't hammer this stuff. It goes to water and dries up quicker'n lightning—an' you hold y'nose an' run. I used it before for the Professor."

Tommy went over to him excitedly. He picked up the little contrivance of many concentric rings. The big motor was throbbing rhythmically, and the generator was humming at the back of the laboratory. Von Holtz was out of sight.

WITH painstaking care Tommy went over the little device. He looked up.

"A coil?"

"I wound one," said Smithers calmly. "On the lathe. Not so hot, but it'll do, I guess. But I can't fix these rings like the Professor did."

"I think I can," said Tommy crisply. "Did you make some wire for springs?"

"Yeah!"

Tommy fingered the wire. Stout, stiff, and surprisingly springy wire of the same peculiar metal. It was that metallic ammonium which chemists have deduced must exist because of the chemical behavior of the compound NH_3, but which Denham alone had managed to procure. Tommy deduced that it was an allotropic modification of the substance which forms an amalgam with mercury, as metallic tin is an allotrope of the amorphous gray powder which is tin in its normal, stable state.

He set to work with feverish excitement. For one hour, for two he worked. At the end of that time he was explaining the matter curtly to Smithers, so intent on his work that he wholly failed to hear a motor car outside or to realize that it had also grown dark in this world of ours.

"You see, Smithers, if a two-dimensional creature wanted to adjust two right angles at right angles to each other, he'd have them laid flat, of course. And if he put a spring at the far ends of those right angles—they'd look like a T, put together—so that the cross-bar of that T was under tension, he'd have the equivalent of what I'm doing. To make a three-dimensioned figure, that imaginary man would have to bend one side of the cross-bar up. As if the two ends of it were under tension by a spring, and the spring would only be relieved of tension when that cross-bar was bent. But the vertical would be his time dimension, so he'd have to have something thin, or it couldn't be bent. He'd need something 'thin in time.'

"We have the same problem. But metallic ammonium is 'thin in time.' It's so fugitive a substance that Denham is the only man ever to secure it. So we use these rings and adjust these springs to them so they're under tension which will only be released when they're all at right angles to each other. In our three dimensions that's impossible, but we have a metal that can revolve in a fourth, and we reinforce their tendency to adjust themselves by starting them off with a jerk. We've got 'em flat. They'll make a good stiff jerk when they try to adjust themselves. And the solenoid's a bit eccentric—"

"Shut up!" snapped Smithers suddenly.

HE was facing the door, bristling. Von Holtz was in the act of coming in, with a beefy, broad-shouldered man with blue jowls. Tommy straightened up, thought swiftly, and then smiled grimly.

"Hullo, Von Holtz," he said pleasantly. "We've just completed a model catapult. We're all set to try it out. Watch!"

He set a little tin can beneath the peculiar device of copper-tubing rings. The can was wholly ordinary, made of thin sheet-iron plated with tin as are all the tin cans of commerce.

"You have the catapult remade?" gasped Von Holtz. "Wait! Wait! Let me look at it!"

For one instant, and one instant only, Tommy let him see. The massed set of concentric rings, each one of them parallel to all the others. It looked rather like a flat coil of tubing; certainly like no particularly obscure form of projector. But as Von Holtz's weak eyes fastened avidly upon it, Tommy pressed the improvised electric switch. At once that would energize the solenoid and release all the tensed springs from their greater tension, for an attempt to reach a permanent equilibrium.

As Von Holtz and the blue-jowled man stared, the little tin can leaped upward into the tiny coil. The small copper rings twinkled one within the other as the springs operated. The tin can was wrenched this way and that, then for the fraction of a second hurt the eyes that gazed upon it—and it was gone! And then the little coil came spinning down to the work bench top from its broken bearings and the remaining copper rings spun aimlessly for a moment. But the third ring of whitish metal had vanished utterly, and so had the coiled-wire springs which Von Holtz had been unable to distinguish. And there was an overpowering smell of ammonia in the room.

VON HOLTZ flung himself upon the still-moving little instrument. He inspected it savagely, desperately. His full red lips drew back in a snarl.

"How did you do it?" he cried shrilly. "You must tell me! I—I—I will kill you if you do not tell me!"

The blue-jowled man was watching Von Holtz. Now his lips twisted disgustedly. He turned to Tommy and narrowed his eyes.

"Look here," he rumbled. "This fool's no good! I want the secret of that trick you did. What's your price?"

"I'm not for sale," said Tommy, smiling faintly.

The blue-jowled man regarded him with level eyes.

"My name's Jacaro," he said after an instant. "Maybe you've heard of me. I'm from Chicago."

Tommy smiled more widely.

"To be sure," he admitted. "You were the man who introduced machine-guns into gang warfare, weren't you? Your gunmen lined up half a dozen of the Buddy Haines gang against a wall and wiped them out, I believe. What do you want this secret for?"

The level eyes narrowed. They looked suddenly deadly.

"That's my business," said Jacaro briefly. "You know who I am. And I want that trick y'did. I got my own reasons. I'll pay for it. Plenty. You know I got plenty to pay, too. Or else—"

"What?"

"Something'll happen to you," said Jacaro briefly. "I ain't sayin' what. But it's damn likely you'll tell what I want to know before it's finished. Name your price and be damn quick!"

Tommy took his hand out of his pocket. He had a gun in it.

"The only possible answer to that," he said suavely, "is to tell you to go to hell. Get out! But Von Holtz stays here. He'd better!"

CHAPTER IV

WITHIN half an hour after Jacaro's leaving, Smithers was in the village, laying in a stock of supplies and sending telegrams that Tommy had written out for transmission. Tommy sat facing an ashen Von Holtz and told him pleasantly what would be done to him if he failed to make the metallic ammonium needed to repair the big solenoid. In an hour, Smithers was back, reporting that Jacaro was also sending telegrams but that he, Smithers, had stood over the telegraph operator until his own messages were transmitted. He brought back weapons, too—highly illegal things to have in New York State, where a citizen is only law-abiding when defenseless. And then four days of hectic, sleepless labor began.

On the first day one of Tommy's friends drove in in answer to a telegram. It was Peter Dalzell, with men in uniform apparently festooned about his car. He announced that a placard warning passersby of smallpox within, had been added to the decorative signs upon the gate, and stared incredulously at the interior of the big brick barn. Tommy grinned at him and gave him plans and specifications of a light steel globe in which two men might be transported into the fifth dimension by a suitably operating device. Tommy had sat up all night drawing those plans. He told Dalzell just enough of what he was up against to enlist Dalzell's enthusiastic cooperation without permitting him to doubt Tommy's sanity. Dalzell had known Tommy as an amateur tennis player, but not as a scientist.

He marveled, refused to believe his eyes when he looked through the dimensoscope, and agreed that the whole thing had to be kept secret or the rescue expedition would be prevented from starting by the incarceration of both Tommy and Smithers in comfortable insane asylums. He feigned to admire Von Holtz, deathly white and nearly frantic with a corroding rage, and complimented Tommy on his taste for illegality. He even asked Von Holtz if he wanted to leave, and Von Holtz snarled insults at him. Von Holtz was beginning to work at the manufacture of metallic ammonium.

IT was an electrolytic process, of course. Ordinarily, when—say—ammonium chloride is broken down by an electric current, ammonium is deposited at the cathode and instantly becomes a gas which dissolves in the water or bubbles up to the surface. With a mercury cathode, it is dissolved and becomes a metallic amalgam, which also breaks down into gas with much bubbling of the mercury. But Denham had worked out a way of delaying the breaking-down, which left him with a curiously white, spongy mass of metal which could be carefully melted down and cast, but not under any circumstances violently struck or strained.

Von Holtz was working at that. On the second day he delivered, snarling, a small ingot of the white metal. He was imprisoned in the lean-to-shed in which the electrolysis went on. But Tommy had more than a suspicion that he was in communication with Jacaro.

"Of course," he said drily to Smithers, who had expressed his doubts. "Jacaro had somebody sneak up and talk to him through the walls, or maybe through a bored hole. While there's a hope of finding out what he wants to know through Von Holtz, Jacaro won't try anything. Not anything rough, anyhow. We mustn't be bumped off while what we are doing is in our heads alone. We're safe enough—for a while."

Smithers grumbled.

"We need that ammonium," said Tommy, "and I don't know how to make it. I bluffed that I could, and in time I might, but it would need time and meanwhile Denham needs us. Dalzell is going to send a plane over today, with word of when we can expect our own globe. We'll try to have the big catapult ready when it comes. And the plane will drop some extra supplies. I've ordered a sub-machine gun. Handy when we get over there in the tree-fern forests. Right now, though, we need to be watching...."

Because they were taking turns looking through the dimensoscope. For signs of Denham and Evelyn. And Tommy was finding himself thinking wholly unscientific thoughts about Evelyn, since a pretty girl in difficulties is of all possible things the one most likely to make a man romantic.

IN the four days of their hardest working, he saw her three times. The globe was wrecked and ruined. Its glass was broken out and its interior ripped apart. It had been pillaged so exhaustively that there was no hope that whatever device had been included in its design, for its return, remained even repairably intact. That device had not worked, to be sure, but Tommy puzzled sometimes over the fact that he had seen no mechanical device of any sort in the plunder that had been brought out to be demolished. But he did not think of those things when he saw Evelyn.

The Ragged Men's encampment was gone, but she and her father lingered furtively, still near the pillaged globe. The first day Tommy saw her, she was still blooming and alert. The second day she was paler. Her clothing was ripped and torn, as if by thorns. Denham had a great raw wound upon his forehead, and his coat was gone and half his shirt was in ribbons. Before Tommy's eyes they killed a nameless small animal with the trunchionlike weapon Evelyn carried. And Denham carted it triumphantly off into the shelter of the tree-fern forest. But to Tommy that shelter began to appear extremely dubious.

That same afternoon some of the Ragged Men came suspiciously to the globe and inspected it, and then vented a gibbering rage upon it with blows and curses. They seemed half-mad, these men. But then, all the Ragged Men seemed a shade less than sane. Their hatred for the Golden City seemed the dominant emotion of their existence.

And when they had gone, Tommy saw Denham peering cautiously from behind a screening mass of fern. And Denham looked sick at heart. His eyes lifted suddenly to the heavens, and he stared off into the distance again, and then he regarded the heavens again with an expression that was at once of the utmost wistfulness and the uttermost of despair.

TOMMY swung the dimensoscope about and searched the skies of that other world. He saw the flying machine, and it was a swallow-winged device that moved swiftly, and now soared and swooped in abrupt short circles almost overhead. Tommy could see its pilot, leaning out to gaze downward. He was no more than a hundred feet up, almost at the height of the tree-fern tops. And the pilot was moving too swiftly for Tommy to be able to focus accurately upon his face, but he could see him as a man, an indubitable man in no fashion distinguishable from the other men of this earth. He was scrutinizing the globe as well as he could without alighting.

He soared upward, suddenly, and his plane dwindled as it went toward the Golden City.

And then, inevitably, Tommy searched for the four Ragged Men who had inspected the globe a little while since. He saw them, capering horribly behind a screening of verdure. They did not shake their clenched fists at the flying machine. Instead, they seemed filled with a ghastly mirth. And suddenly they began to run frantically for the far distance, as if bearing news of infinite importance.

And when he looked back at Denham, it seemed to Tommy that he wrung his hands before he disappeared.

BUT that was the second day of the work upon our own world, and just before sunset there was a droning in the earthly sky above the laboratory, and Tommy ran out, and somebody shot at him from a patch of woodland a quarter of a mile away from the brick building. Isolated as Denham's place was, the shot would go unnoticed. The bullet passed within a few feet of Tommy, but he paid no attention. It was one of Jacaro's watchers, no doubt, but Jacaro did not want Tommy killed. So Tommy waited until the plane swooped low—almost to the level of the laboratory roof—and a thickly padded package thudded to the ground. He picked it up and darted back into the laboratory as other bullets came from the patch of woodland.

"Funny," he said dryly to Smithers, inside the laboratory again; "they don't dare kill me—yet—and Von Holtz doesn't dare leave or refuse to do what I tell him to do; and yet they expect to lick us."

Smithers growled. Tommy was unpacking the wrapped package. A grim, blued-steel thing came out of much padding. Boxes tumbled after it.

"Sub-machine gun," said Tommy, "and ammunition. Jacaro and his little pals will try to get in here when they think we've got the big solenoid ready for use. They'll try to get it before we can use it. This will attend to them."

"An' get us in jail," said Smithers calmly, "for forty-'leven years."

"No," said Tommy, and grinned. "We'll be in the fifth dimension. Our job is to fling through the catapult all the stuff we'll need to make another catapult to fling us back again."

"It can't be done," said Smithers flatly.

"Maybe not," agreed Tommy, "especially since we ruin all our springs and one gymbal ring every time we use the thing. But I've got an idea. I'll want five coils with hollow iron cores, and the whole works shaped like this, with two holes bored so...."

HE sketched. He had been working on the idea for several days, and the sketch was ready in his mind to be transferred to paper.

"What you goin' to do?"

"Something crazy," said Tommy. "A mirror isn't the only thing that changes angles to right ones."

"You're the doctor," said the imperturbable Smithers.

He set to work. He puzzled Tommy sometimes, Smithers did. So far he hadn't asked how much his pay was going to be. He'd worked unintermittantly. He had displayed a colossal, a tremendous calmness. But no man could work as hard as Smithers did without some powerful driving-force. It was on the fourth day that Tommy learned what it was.

The five coils had been made, and Tommy was assembling them with an extraordinary painstaking care behind a screen, to hide what he was doing. He'd discovered a peep-hole bored through the brick wall from the lean-to where Von Holtz worked. He was no longer locked in there. Tommy abandoned the pretense of imprisonment after finding an automatic pistol and a duplicate key to the lock in Von Holtz's possession. He'd had neither when he was theoretically locked up, and Tommy laughed.

"It's a farce, Von Holtz," he said dryly, "this pretending you'll run away. You're here spying now, for Jacaro. Of course. And you don't dare harm either of us until you find out from me what you can't work out for yourself, and know I have done. How much is Jacaro going to pay you for the secret of the catapult, Von Holtz?"

Von Holtz snarled. Smithers moved toward him, his hands closing and unclosing. Von Holtz went gray with terror.

"Talk!" said Smithers.

"A—a million dollars," said Von Holtz, cringing away from the brawny red-headed man.

"It would be interesting to know what use it would be to him," said Tommy dryly. "But to earn that million you have to learn what we know. And to learn that, you have to help us do it again, on the scale we want. You won't run away. So I shan't bother to lock you up hereafter. Jacaro's men come and talk to you at night, don't they?"

VON HOLTZ cringed again. It was an admission.

"I don't want to have to kill any of them," said Tommy pleasantly, "and we'll all be classed as mad if this thing gets out. So you go and talk to them in the lane when you want to, Von Holtz. But if any of them come near the laboratory, Smithers and I will kill them, and if Smithers is hurt I'll kill you; and I don't imagine Jacaro wants that, because he expects you to build another catapult for him. But I warn you, if I find another gun on you I'll thrash you."

Von Holtz's pallor changed subtly from the pallor of fear to the awful lividness of rage.

"You—Gott! You dare threaten—" He choked upon his own fury.

"I do," said Tommy. "And I'll carry out the threat."

Smithers moved forward once more.

"Mr. Von Holtz," he said in a very terrible steadiness, "I aim to kill you some time. I ain't done it yet because Mr. Reames says he needs you a while. But I know you got Miss Evelyn marooned off in them fern-woods on purpose! And—God knows she wouldn't ever look at me, but—I aim to kill you some time!"

His eyes were flames. His hands closed and unclosed horribly. Von Holtz gaped at him, shocked out of his fury into fear again. He went unsteadily back to his lean-to. And Smithers went back to the dimensoscope. It was his turn to watch that other world for signs of Denham and Evelyn, and for any sign of danger to them.

TOMMY adjusted the screen before the bench on which he was working, so Von Holtz could not see his task, and went back to work. It was a rather intricate task he had undertaken, and before the events of the past few days he would have said it was insane. But now he was taking it quite casually.

Presently he said:

"Smithers."

Smithers did not look away from the brass tube.

"Yeah?"

"You're thinking more about Miss Denham than her father."

Smithers did not reply for a moment. Then he said:

"Well? What if I am?"

"I am, too," said Tommy quietly. "I've never spoken to her, and I daresay she's never even heard of me, and she certainly has never seen me, but—"

Smithers said with a vast calmness:

"She'll never look at me, Mr. Reames. I know it. She talks to me, an' laughs with me, but she's never sure-'nough looked at me. An' she never will. But I got the right to love her."

Tommy nodded very gravely.

"Yes. You have. So have I. And so, when that globe comes, we both get into it with what arms and ammunition we can pack in, and go where she is, to help her. I intended to have you work the switch and send me off. But you can come, too."

Smithers was silent. But he took his eyes from the dimensoscope eye-piece and regarded Tommy soberly. Then he nodded and turned back. And it was a compact between the two men that they should serve Evelyn, without any rivalry at all.

TOMMY went on with his work. The essential defect in the catapult Denham had designed was the fact that it practically had to be rebuilt after each use. And, moreover, the metallic ammonium was so fugitive a substance that it was hard to keep. Once it had been strained by working, it gradually adverted to a gaseous state and was lost. And while he still tried to keep the little catapult in a condition for use, he was at no time sure that he could send a pair of automatics and ammunition through in a steel box at any moment that Denham came close enough to notice a burning smoke-fuse attached.

But he was working on another form of catapult entirely, now. In this case he was using hollow magnets placed at known angles to each other. And they were so designed that each one tended to adjust its own hollow bore at right angles to the preceding one, and each one would take any moving, magnetic object and swing it through four successive right angles into the fifth dimension.

He fitted the first magnet on twin rods of malleable copper, which also would carry the current which energized the coil. He threaded the second upon the same twin supports. When the current was passed through the two of them, the magnetic field itself twisted the magnets, bending the copper supports and placing the magnets in their proper relative positions. A third magnet on the same pair of rods, and a repetition of the experiment, proved the accuracy of the idea. And since this device, like the dimensoscope, required only a forty-five degree angle to our known dimensions, instead of a right angle as the other catapult did, Tommy was able to work with ordinary and durable materials. He fitted on the last two coils and turned on the current for his final experiment. And as he watched, the twin three-eighths-inch rods twisted and writhed in the grip of the intangible magnetic force. They bent, and quivered, and twisted…. And suddenly there seemed to be a sort of inaudible *snap*, and one of the magnets hurt the eyes that looked at it, and only the edge of the last of the series was visible.

TOMMY drew in his breath sharply. "Now we try it," he said tensely. "I was trying to work this as the mirrors of the dimensoscope were fitted. Let's see."

He took a long piece of soft-iron wire and fed it into the hollow of the first magnet. He saw it come out and bend stiffly to enter the hollow of the second. It required force to thrust it through. It went still more stiffly into the third magnet. It required nearly all his strength to thrust it on, and on…. The end of it vanished. He pushed two feet or more of it beyond the last place where it was visible. It went into the magnet that hurt one's eyes. After that it could not be seen.

Tommy's voice was strained.

"Swing the dimensoscope, Smithers," he ordered. "See if you can see the wire. The end of it should be in the other world."

It seemed an age, an aeon, that Smithers searched. Then:

"Move it," he said.

Tommy obeyed.

"It's there," said Smithers evenly. "Two or three feet of it."

TOMMY drew a deep, swift breath of relief.

"All right!" he said crisply. "Now we can fling anything we need through there, when our globe arrives. We can built up a dump of supplies, all sent through just before we slide through in the globe."

"Yeah," said Smithers. "Uh—Mr. Reames. There's a bunch of Ragged Men in sight, hauling something heavy behind them. I don't know what it's all about."

Tommy went to the brass tube and stared through it. The tree-fern forest, drawing away in the distance. The vast and steaming morass. The glittering city, far, far in the distance.

And then a mob of the Ragged Men, hauling at some heavy thing. They were a long way off. Some of them came capering on ahead, and Tommy swung the dimensoscope about to see Denham and Evelyn dart for cover and vanish amid the tree-ferns. Denham was as ragged as the Ragged Men, by now, and Evelyn's case was little better.

Frightened for them, Tommy swung the instrument about again. But they had not been seen. The leaders who ran gleefully on ahead were merely in haste. And they were followed more slowly by burly men and lean ones, whole men and limping men, who hauled frantically on long ropes of hide, dragging some heavy thing behind them. Tommy saw it only indistinctly as the filthy, nearly naked bodies moved. But it was an intricate device of a golden-colored metal, and it rested upon the crudest of possible carts. The wheels were sections of tree trunks, pierced for wooden axles. The cart itself was made of the most roughly-hewed of timbers. And there were fifty or more of the Ragged Men who dragged it.

The men in advance now attacked the underbrush at the edge of the forest. They worked with a maniacal energy, clearing away the long fern-fronds while they capered and danced and babbled excitedly.

IRRELEVANTLY, Tommy thought of escaped galley slaves. Just such hard-bitten, vice-ridden men as these, and filled with just such a mad, gibbering hatred of the free men they had escaped from. Certainly these men had been civilized once. As the golden-metal device came nearer, its intricacy was the more apparent. No savages could utilize a device like this one. And there was a queer deadliness in the very grace of its outlines. It was a weapon of some sort, but whose nature Tommy could not even guess.

And then he caught the gleam of metal also in the fern-forest. On the ground. In glimpses and in fragments of glimpses between the swarming naked bodies of the Ragged Men, he pieced together a wholly incredible impression. There was a roadway skirting the edge of the forest. It was not wide; not more than fifteen feet at most. But it was a solid road-bed of metal! The dull silver-white of aluminum gleamed from the ground. Two or more inches thick and fifteen feet wide, there was a seamless ribbon of aluminum that vanished behind the tree-ferns on either side.

The intricate device of golden metal was set up, now, and a shaggy, savage-seeming man mounted beside it grinning. He manipulated its levers and wheels with an expert's assurance. And Tommy saw repairs upon it. Crude repairs, with crude materials, but expertly done. Done by the Ragged Men, past doubt, and so demolishing any idea that they came of a savage race.

"Watch here, Smithers," said Tommy grimly.

HE sat to work upon the little catapult after Denham's design. His own had seemed to work, but the other was more sure. This would be an ambush the Ragged Men were preparing, and of course they would be preparing it for men of the Golden City. The plane had sighted Denham's steel globe. It had hovered overhead, and carried news of what it had seen to the Golden City. And here was a roadway that must have been made by the folk of the Golden City at some time or another. Its existence explained why Denham remained nearby. He had been hoping that some vehicle would travel along its length, containing civilized people to whom he could signal and ultimately explain his plight. And, being near the steel globe, his narrative would have its proofs at hand.

And now it was clear that the Ragged Men expected some ground-vehicle, too. They were preparing for it. They were setting a splendid ambush, with a highly-treasured weapon they ordinarily kept hidden. Their triumphant hatred could apply to nothing else than an expectation of inflicting injury on men of the Golden City.

So Tommy worked swiftly upon the catapult. A new little ring of metallic ammonium was ready, and so were the necessary springs. The Ragged Men would lay their ambush. The men of the Golden City might enter it. They might. But the aviator who had spotted the globe would have seen the shredded contents of the sphere about. He would have known the Ragged Men had found it. And the men who came in a ground-vehicle from the Golden City should be expecting just such an ambush as was being laid.

There would be a fight, and Tommy, somehow, had no doubt that the men of the Golden City would win. And when they had cleared the field he would fling a smoking missile through the catapult. The victors should see it and should examine it. And though writing would serve little purpose, they should at least recognize it as written communication in a language other than their own. And mathematical diagrams would certainly be lucid, and proof of a civilized man sending the missile, and photographs....

THE catapult was ready, and Tommy prepared his message-carrying projectile. He found snapshots and included them. He tore out a photograph of Evelyn and her father, which had been framed above a work bench in the laboratory. He labored, racking his brain for a means of conveying the information that the globe was of any other world.... And suddenly he had an idea. A cord attached to his missile would lead to nothingness from either world, yet one end would be in that other world, and the other end in this. A wire would be better. Tugs upon it would convey the idea of living beings nearby but invisible. The photograph would identify Denham and his daughter as associated with the phenomenon and competent to explain it....

Tommy worked frantically to get the thing ready. He almost prayed that the men of the Golden City would be victors, would find his little missile when the fray was over, and would try to comprehend it....

All he could do was try.

Then Smithers said, from the dimensoscope:

"They're all set, Mr. Reames. Y'better look."

Tommy stared through the eye-piece. Strangely, the golden weapon had vanished. All seemed to be exactly as before. The cleared-away underbrush was replaced. Nothing was in any way changed from the normal in that space upon a mad world. But there was a tiny movement and Tommy saw a Ragged Man. He was lying prone upon the earth. He seemed either to hear or see something, because his lips moved as he spoke to another invisible man beside him, and his expression of malevolent joy was horrible.

Tommy swung the tube about. Nothing.... But suddenly he saw swiftly-moving winkings of sunlight from the edge of the tree-fern forest. Something was moving in there, moving with lightning swiftness along the fifteen-foot roadway of solid aluminum. It drew nearer, and more near....

THE carefully camouflaged ambuscade was fully focussed and Tommy was watching tensely when the thing happened.

He saw glitterings through the tree-fronds come to a smoothly decelerated stop. There was a pause; and suddenly the underbrush fell flat. As if a single hand had smitten it, it wavered, drooped, and lay prone. The golden weapon was exposed, with its brawny and horribly grinning attendant. For one-half a split second Tommy saw the wheeled thing in which half a dozen men of the Golden City were riding. It was graceful and stream-lined and glittering. There was a platform on which the steel sphere would have been mounted for carrying away.

But then there was a sudden intolerable light as the men of the Golden City reached swiftly for peculiar weapons beside them. The light came from the crudely mounted weapon of the Ragged Men, and it was an unbearable actinic glare. For half a second, perhaps, it persisted, and died away to a red flame which leaped upward and was not.

Then the vehicle from the Golden City was a smoking, twisted ruin. Four of the six men in it were blasted, blackened crisps. Another staggered to his feet, struggled to reach a weapon and could not lift it, and twitched a dagger from his belt and fell forward; and Tommy could see that his suicide was deliberate.

The last man, alone, was comparatively unharmed by the blast of light. He swept a pistol-like contrivance into sight. It bore swiftly upon the now surging, yelling horde of Ragged Men. And one—two—three of them seemed to scream convulsively before they were trampled under by the rest.

But suddenly there were a myriad little specks of red all over the body of the man at bay. The pistol-like thing dropped from his grasp as his whole hand became encrimsoned. And then he was buried beneath the hating, blood-lusting mob of the forest men.

CHAPTER V

AN hour later, Tommy took his eyes away from the dimensoscope eye-piece. He could not bear to look any longer.

"Why don't they kill him?" he demanded sickly, filled with a horrible, a monstrous rage. "Oh, why don't they kill him?"

He felt maddeningly impotent. In another world entirely, a mob of half-naked renegades had made a prisoner. He was not dead, that solely surviving man from the Golden City. He was bound, and the Ragged Men guarded him closely, and his guards were diverting themselves unspeakably by small tortures, minor tortures, horribly painful but not weakening. And they capered and howled with glee when the bound man writhed.

The prisoner was a brave man, though. Helpless as he was, he presently flung back his head and set his teeth. Sweat stood out in great droplets upon his body and upon his forehead. And he stilled his writhings, and looked at his captors with a grim and desperate defiance.

The guards made gestures which were all too clear, all too luridly descriptive of the manner of death which awaited him. And the man of the Golden City was ashen and hopeless and utterly despairing—and yet defiant.

Smithers took Tommy's place at the eye-piece of the instrument. His nostrils quivered at what he saw. The vehicle from the Golden City was being plundered, of course. Weapons from the dead men were being squabbled over, even fought over. And the Ragged Men fought as madly among themselves as if in combat with their enemies. The big golden weapon on its cart was already being dragged away to its former hiding-place. And somehow, it was clear that those who dragged it away expected and demanded that the solitary prisoner not be killed until their return.

It was that prisoner, in the agony which was only the beginning of his death, who made Smithers' teeth set tightly.

"I DON'T see the Professor or Miss Evelyn," said Smithers in a vast calmness. "I hope to Gawd they—don't see this."

Tommy swung on his heel, staring and ashen.

"They were near," he said stridently. "I saw them! They saw what happened in the ambush! They'll—they'll see that man tortured!"

Smithers' hand closed and unclosed.

"Maybe the Professor'll have sense enough to take Miss Evelyn—uh—where she—can't hear," he said slowly, his voice level. "I hope so."

Tommy flung out his hands desperately.

"I want to help that man!" he cried savagely. "I want to do something! I saw what they promised to do to him. I want to—to kill him, even! It would be mercy!"

Smithers said, with a queer, stilly shock in his voice:

"I see the Professor now. He's got that gun-thing in his hand.... Miss Evelyn's urging him to try to do something.... He's looking at the sky.... It'll be a long time before it's dark.... He's gone back out of sight...."

"If we had some dynamite!" said Tommy desperately, "we could take a chance on blowing ourselves to bits and try to fling it through and into the middle of those devils...."

HE was pacing up and down the laboratory, harrowed by the fate of that gray-faced man who awaited death by torture; filled with a wild terror that Evelyn and her father would try to rescue him and be caught to share his fate; racked by his utter impotence to do more than watch....

Then Smithers said thickly:

"God!"

He stumbled away from the eye-piece. Tommy took his place, dry-throated with terror. He saw the Ragged Men laughing uproariously. The bearded man who was their leader was breaking the arms and legs of the prisoner so that he would be helpless when released from the stake to which he was bound. And if ever human beings looked like devils out of hell, it was at that moment. The method of breaking the bones was excruciating. The prisoner screamed. The Ragged Men rolled upon the ground in their maniacal mirth.

And then a man dropped, heaving convulsively, and then another, and still another.... The grim, gaunt figure of Denham came out of the tree-fern forest, the queer small golden-metal trunchion in his hand. A fourth man dropped before the Ragged Men quite realized what had happened. The fourth man himself was armed—and a flashing slender body came plunging from the forest and Evelyn flung herself upon the still-heaving body and plucked away that weapon.

TOMMY groaned, in the laboratory in another world. He could not look away, and yet it seemed that the heart would be torn from his body by that sight. Because the Ragged Men had turned upon Denham with a concentrated ferocity, somehow knowing instantly that he was more nearly akin to the men of the Golden City than to them. But at sight of Evelyn, her garments rent by the thorns of the forest, her white body gleaming through the largest tears, they seemed to go mad. And Tommy's eyes, glazing, saw the look on Denham's face as he realized that Evelyn had not fled, but had followed him in his desperate and wholly hopeless effort.

Then the swarming mass of Ragged Men surged over the two of them. Buried them under reaching, hating, lusting fiends who fought even among themselves to be first to seize them.

Then there was only madness, and Denham was bound beside the man of the Golden City, and Evelyn was the center of a fighting group which was suddenly flung aside by the bearded giant, and the encampment of the Ragged Men was bedlam. And somehow Tommy knew with a terrible clarity that a man of the Golden City to torture was bliss unimaginable to these half-mad enemies of that city. But a woman—

He turned from the instrument, three-quarters out of his head. He literally did not see Von Holtz gazing furtively in the doorway. His eyes were fixed and staring. It seemed that his brain would burst.

Then he heard his own voice saying with an altogether unbelievable steadiness:

"Smithers! They've got Evelyn. Get the sub-machine gun."

SMITHERS cried out hoarsely. His face was not quite human, for an instant. But Tommy was bringing the work bench on which he had installed his magnetic catapult, close over by the dimensoscope.

"This cannot work," he said in the same incredible calmness. "Not possibly. It should not work. It will not work. But it has to work!"

He was clamping the catapult to a piece of heavy timber.

"Put the gun so it shoots into the first magnet," he said steadily. "The magnet-windings shouldn't stand the current we've got to put into them. They've got to."

Smithers' fingers were trembling and unsteady. Tommy helped him, not looking through the dimensoscope at all.

"Start the dynamo," he said evenly—and marveled foolishly at the voice that did not seem to belong to him at all, talking so steadily and so quietly. "Give me all the juice you've got. We'll cut out this rheostat."

He was tightening a vise which would hold the deadly little weapon in place while Smithers got the crude-oil engine going and accelerated it recklessly to its highest speed. Tommy flung the switch. Rubber insulation steamed and stank. He pulled the trigger of the little gun for a single shot. The bullet flew into the first hollow magnet, just as he had beforehand thrust an iron wire. It vanished. The series of magnets seemed unharmed.

WITH a peculiar, dreamlike steadiness, Tommy put his hand where an undeflected bullet would go through it. He pressed the trigger again. He felt a tiny breeze upon his hand. But the bullet had been unable to elude the compound-wound magnets, each of which now had quite four times the designed voltage impressed upon its coils.

Tommy flung off the switch.

"Work the gun," he ordered harshly. "When I say fire, send a burst of shots through it. Keep the switch off except when you're actually firing, so—God willing—the coils don't burn out. Fire!"

He was gazing through the dimensoscope. Evelyn was struggling helplessly while two Ragged Men held her arms, grinning as only devils could have grinned, and others squabbled and watched with a fascinated attention some cryptic process which could only be the drawing of lots....

Tommy saw, and paid no attention. The machine-gun beside him rasped suddenly. He saw a tree-fern frond shudder. He saw a gaping, irregular hole where a fresh frond was uncurling. Tommy put out his hand to the gun.

"Let me move it, bench and all," he said steadily. "Now try it again. Just a burst."

AGAIN the gun rasped. And the earth was kicked up suddenly where the bullets struck in that other world. The little steel-jacketed missiles were deflected by the terribly overstrained magnets of the catapult, but their energy was not destroyed. It was merely altered in direction. Fired within the laboratory upon our own and normal world, the bullets came out into the world of tree-ferns and monstrous things. They came out, as it happened, sideways instead of point first, which was due to some queer effect of dimension change upon an object moving at high velocity. Because of that, they ricocheted much more readily, and where they struck they made a much more ghastly wound. But the first two bursts caused no effect at all. They were not even noticed by the Ragged Men. The noise of the little gun was thunderous and snarling in the laboratory, but in the world of the fifth dimension there was no sound at all.

"Like this," said Tommy steadily. "Just like this.... Now fire!"

He had tilted the muzzle upward. And then with a horrible grim intensity he traversed the gun as it roared.

And it was butchery. Three Ragged Men were cut literally to bits before the storm of bullets began to do real damage. The squabbling group, casting lots for Evelyn, had a swathe of dead men in its midst before snarls begun had been completed.

"Again," said Tommy coldly. "Again, Smithers, again!"

AND again the little gun roared. The burly bearded man clutched at his throat—and it was a gory horror. A Thing began to run insanely. It did not even look human any longer. It stumbled over the leader of the Ragged Men and died as he had done. The bullets came tumbling over themselves erratically. They swooped and curved and dispersed themselves crazily.

Spinning as they were, at right angles to their line of flight, their trajectories were incalculable and their impacts were grisly.

The little gun fired ten several bursts, aimed in a desperate cold-bloodedness, before the smell of burnt rubber became suddenly overpowering and the rasping sound of an electric arc broke through the rumbling of the crude-oil engine in the back.

Smithers sobbed.

"Burnt out!"

But Tommy waved his hand.

"I think," he said savagely, "that maybe a dozen of them got away. Evelyn's staggering toward her father. She'll turn him loose. That prisoner's dead, though. Didn't mean to shoot him, but those bullets flew wild."

He gave Smithers the eye-piece. Sweat was rolling down his forehead in great drops. His hands were trembling uncontrollably.

He paced shakenly up and down the laboratory, trying to shut out of his own sight the things he had seen when the bullets of his own aiming literally splashed into the living flesh of men. He had seen Ragged Men disemboweled by those spinning, knifelike projectiles. He had turned a part of the mad world of that other dimension into a shambles, and he did not regret it because he had saved Evelyn, but he wanted to shut out the horror of seeing what he had done.

"But now," he said uncertainly to himself, "they're no better off, except they've got weapons…. If that man from the Golden City hadn't been killed…."

HE was looking at the magnetic catapult, burned out and useless. His eyes swung suddenly to the other one. Just a little while since he had made ready a missile to be thrown through into the other world by that. It contained snapshots, and diagrams, and it was an attempt to communicate with the men of the Golden City without any knowledge of their language.

"But—I can communicate with Denham!"

He began to write feverishly. If he had looked out of the laboratory window, he would have seen Von Holtz running like a deer, waving his arms jerkily, and—when out of earshot of the laboratory—shouting loudly. And Von Holtz was carrying a small black box which Tommy would have identified instantly as a motion picture camera, built for amateurs but capable of taking pictures indoors and with a surprisingly small amount of light. And if Tommy had listened, he might possibly have heard the beginnings of those shoutings to men hidden in a patch of woodland about a quarter of a mile away. The men, of course, were Jacaro's, waiting until either Von Holtz had secured the information that was wanted, or until an assault in force upon the laboratory would net them a catapult ready for use—to be examined, photographed, and duplicated at leisure.

But Tommy neither looked nor listened. He wrote feverishly, saying to Smithers at the dimensoscope:

"Denham'll be looking around to see what killed those men. When he does, we want to be ready to shoot a smoke-bomb through to him, with a message attached."

Smithers made a gesture of no especial meaning save that he had heard. And Tommy went on writing swiftly, saying who he was and what he had done, and that another globe was being built so that he and Smithers could come with supplies and arms to help....

"He's lookin" around now, Mr. Reames," said Smithers quietly. "He's picked up a ricocheted bullet an' is staring at it."

THE crude-oil engine was running at a thunderous rate. Tommy fastened his note in the little missile he had made ready. He placed it under the solenoid of the catapult after Denham's design, with the springs and rings of metallic ammonium. He turned to Smithers.

"I'll watch for him," said Tommy unsteadily. "You know, watch for the right moment to fling it through. Slow up the generator a little. It'll rack itself to pieces."

He put his eye to the eye-piece. He winced as he saw again what the bullets of his aiming had done. But he saw Denham almost at once. And Denham was scratched and bruised and looked very far indeed from the ideal of a professor of theoretic physics, with hardly more than a few shreds of clothing left upon him, and a ten-day's beard upon his face. He limped as he walked. But he had stopped in the task of gathering up weapons to show Evelyn excitedly what it was that he had found. A spent and battered bullet, but indubitably a bullet from the world of his own ken. He began to stare about him, hopeful yet incredulous.

Tommy took his eye from the dimensoscope just long enough to light the fuse of the smoke-bomb.

"Here it goes, Smithers!"

He flung the switch. The missile with its thickly smoking fuse leaped upward as the concentric rings flickered and whirled bewilderingly. The missile hurt the eyes that watched it. It vanished. The solenoid dropped to the floor from the broken small contrivance.

Then Tommy's heart stood still as he gazed through the eye-piece again. He could see nothing but an opaque milkiness. But it drifted away, and he realised that it was smoke. More, Denham was staring at it. More yet, he was moving cautiously towards its source, one of the strange golden weapons held ready....

Denham was investigating.

THE generator at the back of the laboratory slowed down. Smithers was obeying orders. Tommy hung close by the vision instrument, his hands moving vaguely and helplessly, as one makes gestures without volition when anxious for someone else to duplicate the movements for which he sets the example.

He saw Denham, very near, inspecting the smoking thing on the ground suspiciously. The smoke-fuse ceased to burn. Denham stared. After an age-long delay, he picked up the missile Tommy had prepared. And Tommy saw that there was a cord attached to it. He had fastened that cord when planning to try to communicate with the men of the Golden City, when he had expected them to be victorious.

But he saw Denham's face light up with pathetic hope. He called to Evelyn. He hobbled excitedly to her, babbling....

Tommy watched, and his heart pounded suddenly as Evelyn turned and smiled in the direction in which she knew the dimensoscope must be. A huge butterfly, its wings a full yard across, fluttered past her head. Denham talked excitedly to her. A clumsy batlike thing swooped by overhead. Its shadow blanketed her face for an instant. A running animal, small and long, ran swiftly in full view from one side of the dimensoscope's field of vision to the other. Then a snake, curiously horned, went writhing past....

Denham talked excitedly. He turned and made gestures as of writing, toward the spot where he had picked up Tommy's message. He began to search for a charred stick where the Ragged Men had built a fire some days now past. A fleeing furry thing sped across his feet, running....

DENHAM looked up. And Evelyn was staring now. She was staring in the direction of the Golden City. And now what was almost a wave of animals, all wild and all fleeing, swept across the field of vision of the dimensoscope. There were gazelles, it seemed—slender-limbed, graceful animals, at any rate—and there were tiny hoofed things which might have been eohippi, and then a monstrous armadillo clanked and rattled past....

Tommy swung the dimensoscope. He gasped. All the animal world was in flight. The insects had taken to wing. Flying creatures were soaring upward and streaking through the clear blue sky, and all in the one direction. And then out of the morass came monstrous shapes; misshapen, unbelievable reptilian shapes, which fled bellowing thunderously for the tree-fern forest. They were gigantic, those things from the morass. They were hideous. They were things out of nightmares, made into flabby flesh. There were lizards and what might have been gigantic frogs, save that frogs possess no tails. And there were long and snaky necks terminating in infinitesimal heads, and vast palpitating bodies following those impossible small brain-cases, and long tapering tails that thrashed mightily as the ghastly things fled bellowing....

And the cause of the mad panic was a slowly moving white curtain of mist. It was flowing over the marsh, moving with apparent deliberation, but, as Tommy saw, actually very swiftly. It shimmered and quivered and moved onward steadily. Its upper surface gleamed with elusive prismatic colors. It had blotted out the horizon and the Golden City, and it came onward....

DENHAM made frantic, despairing gestures toward the dimensoscope. The thing was coming too fast. There was no time to write. Denham held high the cord that trailed from the message-bearing missile. He gesticulated frantically, and raced to the gutted steel globe and heaved mightily upon it and swung it about so that Tommy saw a great steel ring set in its side, which had been hidden before. He made more gestures, urgently, and motioned Evelyn inside.

Tommy struck at his forehead.

"It's poison gas," he muttered. "Revenge for the smashed-up vehicle.... They knew it by an automatic radio signal, maybe. This is their way of wiping out the Ragged Men.... Poison gas.... It'll kill Denham and Evelyn.... He wants me to do something...."

He drew back, staring, straining every nerve to think.... And somehow his eyes were drawn to the back of the laboratory and he saw Smithers teetering on his feet, with his hands clasped queerly to his body, and a strange man standing in the door of the laboratory with an automatic pistol in his hand. The automatic had a silencer on it, and its clicking had been drowned out, anyhow, by the roaring of the crude-oil engine.

The man was small and dark and natty. His lips were drawn back in a peculiar mirthless grin as Smithers teetered stupidly back and forth and then fell....

The explosion of Tommy's own revolver astounded him as much as it did Jacaro's gunman. He did not ever remember drawing it or aiming. The natty little gunman was blotted out by a spouting mass of white smoke—and suddenly Tommy knew what it was that Denham wanted him to do.

THERE was rope in a loose and untidy coil beneath a work bench. Tommy sprang to it in a queer, nightmarish activity. He knew what was happening, of course. Von Holtz had seen the magnetic catapult at work. That couldn't be destroyed or its workings hidden like the ring catapult of Denham's design. He'd gone out to call in Jacaro's men. And they'd shot down Smithers as a cold-blooded preliminary to the seizure of the instrument Jacaro wanted.

It was necessary to defend the laboratory. But Tommy could not spare the time. That white mist was moving upon Evelyn and her father, in that other world. It was death, as the terror of the wild things demonstrated. They had to be helped....

He knotted the rope to the end of the cord that vanished curiously somewhere among the useless mass of rings. He tugged at the cord—and it was tugged in return. Denham, in another world, had felt his signal and had replied to it....

A window smashed suddenly and a bullet missed Tommy's neck by inches. He fired at that window, and absorbedly guided the knot of the rope past its vanishing point. The knot ceased to exist and the rope crept onward—and suddenly moved more and more swiftly to a place where abruptly it was not. For the length of half an inch, the rope hurt the eyes that looked at it. Beyond that it was not possible to see it at all.

Tommy leaped up. He plunged ahead of two separate spurts of shots from two separate windows. The shots pierced the place where he had been. He was racing for the crude-oil engine. There was a chain wound upon a drum, there, and a clutch attached the drum to the engine.

He stopped and seized the repeating shotgun Smithers had brought as his own weapon against Jacaro's gangsters. He sent four loads of buckshot at the windows of the laboratory. A man yelled.

And Tommy had dropped the gun to knot the rope to the chain, desperately, fiercely, in a terrible haste.

THE chain began to pay out to that peculiar vanishing point which was here an entry-way to another world—perhaps another universe.

A bullet nicked his ribs. He picked up the gun and fired it nearly at random. He saw Smithers moving feebly, and Tommy had a vast compassion for

Smithers, but— He shuddered suddenly. Something had struck him a heavy blow in the shoulder. And something else battered at his leg. There was no sound that could be heard above the thunder of the crude-oil motor, but Tommy, was queerly aware of buzzing things flying about him, and of something very warm flowing down his body and down his leg. And he felt very dizzy and weak and extremely tired.... He could not see clearly, either.

But he had to wait until Denham had the chain fast to the globe. That was the way he had intended to come back, of course. The ring was in the globe, and this chain was in the laboratory to haul the globe back from wherever it had been sent. And Von Holtz had disconnected it before sending away the globe with Denham in it. If the chain remained unbroken, of course it could be hauled in, as it would turn all necessary angles and force the globe to follow those angles, whatever they might be....

Tommy was on his hands and knees, and men were saying savagely:

"Where's that thing, hey? Where's th' thing Jacaro wants?"

He wanted to tell them that they should say if the chain had stopped moving to a place where it ceased to exist, so that he could throw a clutch and bring Denham and his daughter back from the place where Von Holtz had marooned them when he wanted to steal Denham's secret. Tommy wanted to explain that. But the floor struck him in the face, and something said to him:

"They've shot you."

BUT it did not seem to matter, somehow, and he lay very still until he felt himself strangling, and he was breathing in strong ammonia which made his eyes smart and his tired lungs gasp.

Then he saw flames, and heard a motor car roaring away from close by the laboratory.

"They've stolen the catapult and set fire to the place," he remembered dizzily, "and now they're skipping out...."

Even that did not seem to matter. But then he heard the chain clank, next to him on the floor. The white mist! Denham and Evelyn waiting for the white mist to reach them, and Denham jerking desperately on the chain to signal that he was ready....

The flames had released ammonia from the metal Von Holtz had made. That had roused Tommy. But it did not give him strength. It is impossible to say where Tommy's strength came from, when somehow he crawled to the clutch lever, with the engine roaring steadily above him, and got one hand on the lever, and edged himself up, and up, and up, until he could swing his whole weight on that lever. That instant of dangling hurt excruciatingly, too, and Tommy saw only that the drum began to revolve swiftly, winding the chain upon it, before his grip gave way.

And the chain came winding in and in from nowhere, and the tall laboratory filled more and more thickly with smoke, and lurid flames appeared somewhere, and a rushing sound began to be audible as the fire roared upward to the inflammable roof, and the engine ran thunderously....

THEN, suddenly, there was a shape in the middle of the laboratory floor. A huge globular shape which it hurt the eyes to look upon. It became visible out of nowhere as if evoked by magic amid the flames of hell. But it came, and was solid and substantial, and it slid along the floor upon small wheels until it wound up with a crash against the winding drum, and the chain shrieked as it tightened unbearably—and the engine choked and died.

Then a door opened in the monstrous globe. Two figures leaped out, aghast. Two ragged, tattered, strangely-armed figures, who cried out to each other and started for the door. But the girl stumbled over Tommy and called, choking, to her father. Groping toward her, he found Smithers. And then Tommy smiled drowsily to himself as soft arms tugged bravely at him, and a slender, glorious figure staggered with him to fresh air.

"It's Von Holtz," snapped Denham, and coughed as he fought his way to the open. "I'll blast him to hell with these things we brought back...."

THAT was the last thing Tommy knew until he woke up in bed with a feeling of many bandages and an impression that his lungs hurt.

Denham seemed to have heard him move. He looked in the door.

"Hullo, Reames. You're all right now."

Tommy regarded him curiously until he realized. Denham was shaved and fully clothed. That was the strangeness about him. Tommy had been watching him for many days as his clothing swiftly deteriorated and his beard grew.

"You are, too, I see," he said weakly. "I'm damned glad." Then he felt foolish, and querulous, and as if he should make some apology, and instead said, "But five dimensions does seem extreme. Three is enough for ordinary use, and four is luxurious. Five seems to be going a bit too far."

Denham blinked, and then grinned suddenly. Tommy had admired the man who could face so extraordinary a situation with such dogged courage, and now he found, suddenly, that he liked Denham.

"Not too far," said Denham grimly. "Look!" He held up one of the weapons Tommy had seen in that other world, one of the golden-colored truncheons. "I brought this back. The same metal they built that wagon of theirs with. All their weapons. Most of their tools—as I know. It's gold, man! They use gold in that world as we use steel here. That's why Jacaro was ready to kill to get the secret of getting there. Von Holtz enlisted him."

"How did you know—" began Tommy weakly.

"Smithers," said Denham. "We dragged both of you out before the lab went-up in smoke. He's going to be all right, too. Evelyn's nursing both of you. She wants to talk to you, but I want to say this first: You did a damned fine thing, Reames! The only man who could have saved us, and you just about killed yourself doing it. Smithers saw you swing that clutch lever with three bullets in your body. And you're a scientist, too. You're my partner, Reames, in what we do in the fifth dimension."

TOMMY blinked. "But five dimensions does seem extreme...."

"We are the Interdimensional Trading Company," said Denham, smiling. "Somehow, I think we'll find something in this world we can trade for the gold in that. And we've got to get there, Reames, because Jacaro will surely try to make use of that catapult principle you worked out. He'll raise the devil; and I think the people of that Golden City would be worth knowing. No, we're partners. Sooner or later, you'll know how I feel about what you've done. I'm going to bring Evelyn in here now."

He vanished. An instant later Tommy heard a voice—a girl's voice. His heart began to pound. Denham came back into the room and with him was Evelyn. She smiled warmly upon Tommy, though as his eyes fell blankly upon the smart sport clothes she was again wearing, she flushed.

"My daughter Evelyn," said Denham. "She wants to thank you."

And Tommy felt a warm soft hand pressing his, and he looked deep into the eyes of the girl he had never before spoken to, but for whom he had risked his life, and whom he knew he would love forever. There were a thousand things crowding to his lips for utterance. He had watched Evelyn, and he loved her—

"H-how do you do?" said Tommy, lamely. "I'm—awfully glad to meet you."

But before he was well he learned to talk more sensibly.

—And the ships, at that touch, fell helplessly down from the heights.

THE PIRATE PLANET

PART THREE OF A FOUR-PART NOVEL

By Charles W. Diffin

> Two fighting Yankees—war-torn Earth's sole representatives on Venus—set out to spike the greatest gun of all time.

WHAT HAS GONE BEFORE

THE attack comes without warning; its reason is unknown. But Venus is approaching the earth, and flashes from the planet are followed by terrific explosions that wreak havoc throughout the world. Lieutenant McGuire and Captain Blake of the U. S. Army Air Service see a great ship fly in from space. Blake attacks it with the 91st Squadron in support, and Blake alone survives. McGuire and Professor Sykes, an astronomer of Mount Lawson, are captured.

The bombardment ceases as Venus passes on, and the people of Earth sink into hopeless despondency. Less than a year and a half and the planet will return, and then—the end! The armament of Earth is futile against an enemy who has conquered space. Blake hopes that science might provide a means; might show our fighters how to go out into space and throttle the attack at its source. But the hope is blasted, until a radio from McGuire supplies a lead.

McGuire is on Venus. He and Sykes land on that distant planet, captives of a barbarous people. They are taken before Torg, the emperor, and his council, and they learn that these red, man-shaped beasts intend to conquer the earth. Spawning in millions, they are crowded, and Earth is to be their colony.

Imprisoned on a distant island, the two captives are drugged and hypnotized before a machine which throws their thoughts upon a screen. Involuntary traitors, they disclose the secrets of Earth and its helplessness; then attempt to escape and end their lives rather than be forced to further betrayal of their own people.

McGuire finds a radio station and sends a message back to Earth. He implores Blake to find a man named Winslow, for Winslow has invented a space ship and claims to have reached the moon.

No time for further sending—McGuire does not even know if his message has been received—but they reach the ocean where death offers them release. A force of their captors attacking on land, they throw themselves from a cliff, then swim out to drown beyond reach in the ocean. An enemy ship sweeps above them: its gas cloud threatens not the death they desire but unconsciousness and capture. "God help us," says Sykes; "we can't even die!"

They sink, only to be buoyed up by a huge metal shape. A metal projector raises from the ocean, bears upon the enemy ship and sends it, a mass of flame and molten metal, into the sea. And friendly voices are in McGuire's ears as careful hands lift the two men and carry them within the craft that has saved them.

CHAPTER XIII

LIEUTENANT MCGUIRE had tried to die. He and Professor Sykes had welcomed death with open arms, and death had been thwarted by their enemies who wanted them alive—wanted to draw their knowledge from them as a vampire bat might seek to feast. And, when even death was denied them, help had come.

The enemy ship had gone crashing to destruction where its melting metal made hissing clouds of steam as it buried itself in the ocean. And this craft that had saved them—Lieutenant McGuire had never been on a submarine, but he knew it could be only that that held him now and carried him somewhere at tremendous speed.

This was miracle enough! But to see, with eyes which could not be deceiving him, a vision of men, human, white of face—men like himself—bending and working over Sykes' unconscious body—that could not be immediately grasped.

Their faces, unlike the bleached-blood horrors he had seen, were aglow with the flush of health. They were tall, slenderly built, graceful in their quick motions as they worked to revive the unconscious man. One stopped, as he passed, to lay a cool hand on McGuire's forehead, and the eyes that looked down seemed filled with the blessed quality of kindness.

They were human—his own kind!—and McGuire was unable to take in at first the full wonder of it.

Did the tall man speak? His lips did not move, yet McGuire heard the words as in some inner ear.

"We were awaiting you, friend Mack Guire." The voice was musical, thrilling, and yet the listening man could not have sworn that he heard a voice at all. It was as if a thought were placed within his mind by the one beside him.

The one who had paused hurried on to aid the others, and McGuire let his gaze wander.

THE porthole beside him showed dimly a pale green light; they were submerged, and the hissing rush of water told him that they were travelling fast. There was a door in the farther wall; beyond was a room of gleaming lights that reflected from myriads of shining levers and dials. A control room. A figure moved as McGuire watched, to press on a lever where a red light was steadily increasing in brightness. He consulted strange instruments before him, touched a metal button here and there, then opened a switch, and the rippling hiss of waters outside their craft softened to a gentler note.

The tall one was beside him again.

"Your friend will live," he told him in that wordless tongue, "and we are almost arrived. The invisible arms of our anchorage have us now and will draw us safely to rest."

The kindly tone was music in McGuire's ears, and he smiled in reply. "Friends!" he thought. "We are among friends."

"You are most welcome," the other assured him, "and, yes, you are truly among friends." But the lieutenant glanced upward in wonder, for he knew that he had uttered no spoken word.

Their ship turned and changed its course beneath them, then came finally to rest with a slight rocking motion as if cushioned on powerful springs. Sykes was being assisted to his feet as the tall man reached for McGuire's hand and helped him to rise.

The two men of Earth stood for a long minute while they stared unbelievingly into each other's eyes. Their wonder and amazement found no words for expression but must have been apparent to the one beside them.

"You will understand," he told them. "Do not question this reality even to yourselves. You are safe!... Come." And he led the way through an opening doorway to a wet deck outside. Beyond this was a wharf of carved stone, and the men followed where steps were inset to allow them to ascend.

Again McGuire could not know if he heard a tumult of sound or sensed it in some deeper way. The air about them was aglow with soft light, and it echoed in his ears with music unmistakably real—beautiful music!—exhilarating! But the clamor of welcoming voices, like the words from their tall companion, came soundlessly to him.

THERE were people, throngs of them, waiting. Tall like the others, garbed, like those horrible beings of a past that seemed distant and remote, in loose garments of radiant colors. And everywhere were welcoming smiles and warm and friendly glances.

McGuire let his dazed eyes roam around to find the sculptured walls of a huge room like a tremendous cave. The soft glow of light was everywhere, and it brought out the beauty of flowing lines and delicate colors in statuary and bas-relief that adorned the walls. Behind him the water made a dark pool, and from it projected the upper works of their strange craft.

His eyes were hungry for these new sights, but he turned with Sykes to follow their guide through the colorful crowd that parted to let them through. They passed under a carved archway and found themselves in another and greater room.

But was it a room? McGuire marveled at its tremendous size. His eyes took in the smooth green of a grassy lawn, the flowers and plants, and then they followed where the hand of Sykes was pointing. The astronomer gripped McGuire's arm in a numbing clutch; his other hand was raised above.

"The stars," he said. "The clouds are gone; it is night!"

And where he pointed was a vault of black velvet. Deep hues of blue seemed blended with it, and far in its depths were the old familiar star-groups of the skies. "Ah!" the scientist breathed, "the beautiful, friendly stars!"

Their guide waited; then, "Come," he urged gently, and led them toward a lake whose unruffled glassy surface mirrored the stars above. Beside it a man was waiting to receive them.

McGuire had to force his eyes away from the unreal beauty of opal walls like the fairy structures they had seen. There was color everywhere that blended and fused to make glorious harmony that was pure joy to the eyes.

THE man who waited was young. He stood erect, his face like that of a Grecian statue, and his robe was blazing with the flash of jewels. Beside him was a girl, tall and slender, and sweetly serious of face. Like the man, her garments were lovely with jeweled iridescence, and now McGuire saw that the throng within the vast space was similarly apparelled.

The tall man raised his hand.

"Welcome!" he said, and McGuire realized with a start that the words were spoken aloud. "You are most welcome, my friends, among the people of that world you call Venus."

Professor Sykes was still weak from his ordeal; he wavered perceptibly where he stood, and the man before them them turned to give an order. There were chairs that came like magic; bright robes covered them; and the men were seated while the man and girl also took seats beside them as those who prepare for an intimate talk with friends.

Lieutenant McGuire found his voice at last. "Who are you?" he asked in wondering tones. "What does it mean? We were lost—and you saved us. But you—you are not like the others." And he repeated, "What does it mean?"

"No," said the other with a slight smile, "we truly are not like those others. They are not men such as you and I. They are something less than human: animals—vermin!—from whom God, in His wisdom, has seen fit to withhold the virtues that raise men higher than the beasts."

His face hardened as he spoke and for a moment the eyes were stern, but he smiled again as he continued.

"And we," he said, "you ask who we are. We are the people of Venus. I am Djorn, ruler, in name, of all. 'In name' I say, for we rule here by common reason; I am only selected to serve. And this is my sister, Althora. The name, with us, means 'radiant light.'" He turned to exchange smiles with the girl at his side. "We think her well named," he said.

"The others,"—he waved toward the throng that clustered about—"you will learn to know in time."

PROFESSOR SYKES felt the need of introductions.

"This is Lieutenant—" he began, but the other interrupted with an upraised hand.

"Mack Guire," he supplied; "and you are Professor Sykes…. Oh, we know you!" he laughed; "we have been watching you since your arrival; we have been waiting to help you."

The professor was open-mouthed.

"Your thoughts," explained the other, "are as a printed page. We have been with you by mental contact at all times. We could hear, but, at that distance, and—pardon me!—with your limited receptivity, we could not communicate.

"Do not resent our intrusion," he added; "we listened only for our own good, and we shall show you how to insulate your thoughts. We do not pry."

Lieutenant McGuire waved all that aside. "You saved us from them," he said; "that's the answer. But—what does it mean? Those others are in control; they are attacking our Earth, the world where we lived. Why do you permit—?"

Again the other's face was set in sterner lines.

"Yes," he said, and his voice was full of unspoken regret, "they do rule this world; they *have* attacked your Earth; they intend much more, and I fear they must be successful. Listen. Your wonderment is natural, and I shall explain.

"We are the people of Venus. Some centuries ago we ruled this world. Now you find us a handful only, living like moles in this underworld."

"Underworld?" protested Professor Sykes. He pointed above to the familiar constellations. "Where are the clouds?" he asked.

The girl, Althora, leaned forward now. "It will please my brother," she said in a soft voice, "that you thought it real. He has had pleasure in creating that—a replica of the skies we used to know before the coming of the clouds."

PROFESSOR SYKES was bewildered. "That sky—the stars—they are not real?" he asked incredulously. "But the grass—the flowers—"

Her laugh rippled like music. "Oh, they are real," she told him, and her brother gave added explanation.

"The lights," he said: "we supply the actinic rays that the clouds cut off above. We have sunlight here, made by our own hands; that is why we are as we are and not like the red ones with their bleached skins. We had our lights everywhere through the world when we lived above, but those red beasts are ignorant; they do not know how to operate them; they do not know that they live in darkness even in the light."

"Then we are below ground?" asked the flyer. "You live here?"

"It is all we have now. At that time of which I tell, it was the red ones who lived out of sight; they were a race of rodents in human form. They lived in the subterranean caves with which this planet is pierced. We could have exterminated them at any time, but, in our ignorance, we permitted them to live, for we, of Venus—I use your name for the planet—do not willingly take life."

"They have no such compunctions!" Professor Sykes' voice was harsh; he was remembering the sacrifice to the hungry plants.

A flash as of pain crossed the sensitive features of the girl, and the man beside her seemed speaking to her in soundless words.

"Your mind-picture was not pleasant," he told the scientist; then continued:

"Remember, we were upon the world, and these others were within it. There came a comet. Oh, our astronomers plotted its course; they told us we were safe. But at the last some unknown influence diverted it; its gaseous projection swept our world with flame. Only an instant; but when it had passed there was left only death...."

HE was lost in recollection for a time; the girl beside him reached over to touch his hand.

"Those within—the red ones—escaped," he went on. "They poured forth when they found that catastrophe had overwhelmed us. And we, the handful that were left, were forced to take shelter here. We have lived here since, waiting for the day when the Master of Destinies shall give us freedom and a world in which to live."

"You speak," suggested the scientist, "as if this had happened to you. Surely you refer to your ancestors; you are the descendants of those who were saved."

"We are the people," said the other. "We lived then; we live now; we shall live for a future of endless years.

"Have you not searched for the means to control the life principle—you people of Earth?" he asked. "We have it here. You see"—and he waved a hand toward the standing throng—"we are young to your eyes and the others who greeted you were the same."

McGuire and the scientist exchanged glances of corroboration.

"But your age," asked Sykes, "measured in years?"

"We hardly measure life in years."

Professor Sykes nodded slowly; his mind found difficulty in accepting so astounding a fact. "But our language?" he queried. "How is it that you can speak our tongue?"

The tall man smiled and leaned forward to place a hand on a knee of each of the men beside him. "Why not," he asked, "when there doubtless is relationship between us.

"You called the continent Atlantis. Perhaps its very existence is but a fable now: it has been many centuries since we have had instruments to record thought force from Earth, and we have lost touch. But, my friends, even then we of Venus had conquered space, and it was we who visited Atlantis to find a race more nearly like ourselves than were the barbarians who held the other parts of Earth.

"I was there, but I returned. There were some who stayed and they were lost with the others in the terrible cataclysm that sank a whole continent beneath the waters. But some, we have believed, escaped."

"Why have you not been back?" the flyer asked. "You could have helped us so much."

"It was then that our own destruction came upon us. The same comet, perhaps, may have caused a change of stresses in your Earth and sunk the lost Atlantis. Ah! That was a beautiful land, but we have never seen it since. We have been—here.

"But you will understand, now," he added, "that, with our insight into your minds, we have little difficulty in mastering your language."

This talk of science and incredible history left Lieutenant McGuire cold. His mind could not wander long from its greatest concern.

"But the earth!" he exclaimed. "What about the earth? This attack! Those devils mean real mischief!"

"More than you know; more than you can realize, friend Mack Guire!"

"Why?" demanded the flyer. "Why?"

"Have your countries not reached out for other countries when land was needed?" asked the man, Djorn. "Land—land! Space in which to breed—that is the reason for the invasion.

"This world has no such continents as yours. Here the globe is covered by the oceans; we have perhaps one hundredth of the land areas of your Earth And the red ones breed like flies. Life means nothing to them; they die like flies, too. But they need more room; they intend to find it on your world."

"A STRANGE race," mused Professor Sykes. "They puzzled me. But—'less than human,' I think you said. Then how about their ships? How could they invent them?"

"Ours—all ours! They found a world ready and waiting for them. Through the centuries they have learned to master some few of our inventions. The ships!—the ethereal vibrations! Oh, they have been cleverer than we dreamed possible."

"Well, how can we stop them?" demanded McGuire. "We must. You have the submarines—"

"One only," the other interrupted. "We saved that, and we brought some machinery. We have made this place habitable; we have not been idle. But there are limitations."

"But your ray that you projected—it brought down their ship!"

"We were protecting you, and we protect ourselves; that is enough. There is One will deliver us in His own good time; we may not go forth and slaughter."

There was a note of resignation and patience in the voice that filled McGuire with hopeless forebodings. Plainly this was not an aggressive race. They had evolved beyond the stage of wanton slaughter, and, even now, they waited patiently for the day when some greater force should come to their aid.

The man beside them spoke quickly. "One moment—you will pardon me—someone is calling—" He listened intently to some soundless call, and he sent a silent message in reply.

"I have instructed them," he said. "Come and you shall see how impregnable is our position. The red ones have resented our destruction of their ship."

The face of the girl, Althora, was perturbed. "More killings?" she asked.

"Only as they force themselves to their own death," her brother told her. "Be not disturbed."

THE throng in the vast space drew apart as the figure of their leader strode quickly through with the two men following close. There were many rooms and passages; the men had glimpses of living quarters, of places where machinery made soft whirring sounds; more sights than their eyes could see or their minds comprehend. They came at last to an open chamber.

The men looked up to see above them a tremendous inverted-cone, and there was the gold of cloudland glowing through an opening at the top. It was the inside of a volcano where they stood, and McGuire remembered the island and its volcanic peak where the ship had swerved aside. He felt that he knew now where they were.

Above them, a flash of light marked the passage of a ship over the crater's mouth, and he realized that the ships of the reds were not avoiding the island now. Did it mean an attack? And how could these new friends meet it?

Before them on the level volcanic floor were great machines that came suddenly to life, and their roar rose to a thunder of violence, while, in the center, a cluster of electric sparks like whirling stars formed a cloud of blue fire. It grew, and its hissing, crackling length reached upward to a fine-drawn point that touched the opening above.

"Follow!" commanded their leader and went rapidly before them where a passage wound and twisted to bring them at last to the light of day.

The flame of the golden clouds was above them in the midday sky, and beneath it were scores of ships that swept in formations through the air.

"Attacking?" asked the lieutenant with ill-concealed excitement.

"I fear so. They tried to gas us some centuries ago; it may be they have forgotten what we taught them then."

ONE squadron came downward and swept with inconceivable speed over a portion of the island that stretched below. The men were a short distance up on the mountain's side, and the scene that lay before them was crystal clear. There were billowing clouds of gas that spread over the land where the ships had passed. Other ships followed; they would blanket the island in gas.

The man beside them gave a sigh of regret. "They have struck the first blow," he said. He stood silent with half-closed eyes; then: "I have ordered resistance." And there was genuine sorrow and regret in his eyes as he looked toward the mountain top.

McGuire's eyes followed the other's gaze to find nothing at first save the volcanic peak in hard outline upon the background of gold; then only a shimmer as of heat about the lofty cone. The air above him quivered, formed to ripples that spread in great circles where the enemy ships were flashing away.

Swifter than swift aircraft, with a speed that shattered space, they reached out and touched—and the ships, at that touch, fell helplessly down from the heights. They turned awkwardly as they fell or dropped like huge pointed projectiles. And the waters below took them silently and buried in their depths all trace of what an instant sooner had been an argosy of the air.

The ripples ceased, again the air was clear and untroubled, but beneath the golden clouds was no single sign of life.

THE flyer's breathless suspense ended in an explosive gasp. "What a washout!" he exclaimed, and again he thought only of this as a weapon to be used for his own ends. "Can we use that on their fleets?" he asked. "Why, man—they will never conquer the earth; they will never even make a start."

The tall figure of Djorn turned and looked at him. "The lust to kill!" he said sadly. "You still have it—though you are fighting for your own, which is some excuse.

"No, this will not destroy their fleets, for their fleets will not come here to be destroyed. It will be many centuries before ever again the aircraft of the reds dare venture near."

"We will build another one and take it where they are—" The voice of the fighting man was vibrant with sudden hope.

"We were two hundred years building and perfecting this," the other told him. "Can you wait that long?"

And Lieutenant McGuire, as he followed dejectedly behind the leader, heard nothing of Professor Sykes' eager questions as to how this miracle was done.

"Can you wait that long?" this man, Djorn, had asked. And the flyer saw plainly the answer that spelled death and destruction to the world.

CHAPTER XIV

THE mountains of Nevada are not noted for their safe and easy landing places. But the motor of the plane that Captain Blake was piloting roared smoothly in the cool air while the man's eyes went searching, searching, for something, and he hardly knew what that something might be.

He went over again, as he had done a score of times, the remarks of Lieutenant McGuire. Mac had laughed that day when he told Blake of his experience.

"I was flying that transport," he had said, "and, boy! when one motor began to throw oil I knew I was out of luck. Nothing but rocky peaks and valleys full of trees as thick and as pointed as a porcupine's quills. Flying pretty high to maintain altitude with one motor out, so I just naturally *had* to find a place to set her down. I found it, too, though it seemed too good to be true off in that wilderness.

"A fine level spot, all smooth rock, except for a few clumps of grass, and just bumpy enough to make the landing interesting. But, say, Captain! I almost cracked up at that, I was so darn busy staring at something else.

"Off in some trees was a dirigible—Sure; go ahead and laugh; I didn't believe it either, and I was looking at it. But there had been a whale of a storm through there the day before, and it had knocked over some trees that had been screening the thing, and there it was!

"Well, I came to in time to pull up her nose and miss a rock or two, and then I started pronto for that valley of trees and the thing that was buried among them."

CAPTAIN BLAKE recalled the conversation word for word, though he had treated it jokingly at the time. McGuire had found the ship and a man—a half-crazed nut, so it seemed—living there all alone. And he wasn't a bit keen about Mac's learning of the ship. But leave it to Mac to get the facts—or what the old bird claimed were facts.

There was the body of a youngster there, a man of about Mac's age. He had fallen and been killed the day before, and the old man was half crazy with grief. Mac had dug a grave and helped bury the body, and after that the old fellow's story had come out.

He had been to the moon, he said. And this was a space ship. Wouldn't tell how it operated, and shut up like a clam when Mac asked if he had gone alone. The young chap had gone with him, it seemed, and the man wouldn't talk—just sat and stared out at the yellow mound where the youngster was buried.

Mac had told Blake how he argued with the man to prove up on his claims and make a fortune for himself. But no—fortunes didn't interest him. And there were some this-and-that and be-damned-to-'em people who would never get *this* invention—the dirty, thieving rats!

And Mac, while he laughed, had seemed half to believe it. Said the old cuss was so sincere, and he had nothing to sell. And—there was the ship! It never got there without being flown in, that was a cinch. And there wasn't a propellor on it nor a place for one—just open ports where a blast came out, or so the inventor said.

Captain Blake swung his ship on another slanting line and continued to comb the country for such marks as McGuire had seen. And one moment he told himself he was a fool to be on any such hunt, while the next thought would remind him that Mac had believed. And Mac had a level head, and he had radioed from Venus!

There was the thing that made anything seem possible. Mac had got a message through, across that space, and the enemy had ships that could do it. Why not this one?

And always his eyes were searching, searching, for a level rocky expanse and a tree-filled valley beyond, with something, it might be, shining there, unless the inventor had camouflaged it more carefully now.

IT was later on the same day when Captain Blake's blocky figure climbed over the side of the cockpit. Tired? Yes! But who could think of cramped limbs and weary muscles when his plane was resting on a broad, level expanse of rock in the high Sierras and a sharp-cut valley showed thick with pines beyond. He could see the corner only of a rough log shack that protruded.

Blake scrambled over a natural rampart of broken stone and went swiftly toward the cabin. But he stopped abruptly at the sound of a harsh voice.

"Stop where you are," the voice ordered, "and stick up your hands! Then turn around and get back as fast as you can to that plane of yours." There was a glint of sunlight on a rifle barrel in the window of the cabin.

Captain Blake stopped, but he did not turn. "Are you Mr. Winslow?" he asked.

"That's nothing to you! Get out! Quick!"

Blake was thinking fast. Here was the man, without doubt—and he was hostile as an Apache; the man behind that harsh voice meant business. How could he reach him? The inspiration came at once. McGuire was the key.

"If you're Winslow," he called in a steady voice, "you don't want me to go away; you want to talk with me. There's a young friend of yours in a bad jam. You are the only one who can help."

"I haven't any friends," said the rasping voice: "I don't want any! Get out!"

"You had one," said the captain, "whether you wanted him or not. He believed in you—like the other young chap who went with you to the moon."

THERE was an audible gasp of dismay from the window beyond, and the barrel of the rifle made trembling flickerings in the sun.

"You mean the flyer?" asked the voice, and it seemed to have lost its harsher note. "The pleasant young fellow?"

"I mean McGuire, who helped give decent burial to your friend. And now he has been carried off—out into space—and you can help him. If you've a spark of decency in you, you will hear what I have to say."

The rifle vanished within the cabin; a door opened to frame a picture of a tall man. He was stooped; the years, or solitude, perhaps, had borne heavily upon him; his face was a mat of gray beard that was a continuation of the unkempt hair above. The rifle was still in his hand.

But he motioned to the waiting man, and "Come in!" he commanded. "I'll soon know if you're telling the truth. God help you if you're not.... Come in."

An hour was needed while the bearded man learned the truth. And Blake, too, picked up some facts. He learned to his great surprise that he was talking with an educated man, one who had spent a lifetime in scientific pursuits. And now, as the figure before him seemed more the scientist and less the crazed fabricator of wild fancies, the truth of his claims seemed not so remote.

Half demented now, beyond a doubt! A lifetime of disappointments and one invention after another stolen from him by those who knew more of law than of science. And now he held fortune in the secret of his ship—a secret which he swore should never be given to the world.

"Damn the world!" he snarled. "Did the world ever give anything to me? And what would they do with this? They would prostitute it to their own selfish ends; it would be just one more means to conquer and kill; and the capitalists would have it in their own dirty hands so that new lines of transportation beyond anything they dared dream would be theirs to exploit."

BLAKE, remembering the history of a commercial age, found no ready reply to that. But he told the man of McGuire and the things that had made him captive; he related what he, himself, had seen in the dark night on Mount Lawson, and he told of the fragmentary message that showed McGuire was still alive.

"There's only one way to save him," he urged. "If your ship is what you claim it is—and I believe you one hundred per cent—it is all that can save him from what will undoubtedly be a horrible death. Those things were monsters—inhuman!—and they have bombarded the earth. They will come back in less than a year and a half to destroy us."

Captain Blake would have said he was no debater, but the argument and persuasion that he used that night would have done credit to a Socrates. His opponent was difficult to convince, and not till the next day did the inventor show Blake his ship.

"Small," he said as he led the flyer toward it. "Designed just for the moon trip, and I had meant to go alone. But it served; it took us there and back again."

He threw open a door in the side of the metal cylinder. Blake stood back for only a moment to size up the machine, to observe its smooth duralumin shell and the rounded ends where portholes opened for the expelling of its driving blast. The door opening showed a thick wall that gave insulation. Blake followed the inventor to the interior of the ship.

THE man had seen Winslow examining the thick walls. "It's cold out there, you know," he said, and smiled in recollection, "but the generator kept us warm." He pointed to a simple cylindrical casting aft of the ship's center part. It was massive, and braced to the framework of the ship to distribute a thrust that Blake knew must be tremendous. Heavy conduits took the blast that it produced and poured it from ports at bow and stern. There were other outlets, too, above and below and on the sides, and electric controls that were manipulated from a central board.

"You've got a ship," Blake admitted, "and it's a beauty. I know construction, and you've got it here. But what is the power? How do you drive it? What throws it out through space?"

"Aside from one other, you will be the only man ever to know." The bearded man was quiet now and earnest. The wild light had faded from his eyes, and he pondered gravely in making the last and final decision.

"Yes, you shall have it. It may be I have been mistaken. I have known people—some few—who were kindly and decent; I have let the others prejudice me. But there was one who was my companion—and there was McGuire, who was kind and who believed. And now you, who will give your life for a friend and to save humanity!... You shall have it. You shall have the ship! But I will not go with you. I want nothing of glory or fame, and I am too old to fight. My remaining years I choose to spend out here." He pointed where a window of heavy glass showed the outer world and a grave on a sloping hill.

"BUT you shall have full instructions. And, for the present, you may know that it is a continuous explosion that drives the ship. I have learned to decompose water into its components and split them into subatomic form. They reunite to give something other than matter. It is a liquid—liquid energy, though the term is inaccurate—that separates out in two forms, and a fluid ounce of each is the product of thousands of tons of water. The potential energy is all there. A current releases it; the energy components reunite to give matter again—hydrogen and oxygen gas. Combustion adds to their volume through heat.

"It is like firing a cannon in there,"—he pointed now to the massive generator—"a super-cannon of tremendous force and a cannon that fires continuously. The endless pressure of expansion gives the thrust that means a constant acceleration of motion out there where gravity is lost.

"You will note," he added, "that I said 'constant acceleration.' It means building up to speeds that are enormous."

Blake nodded in half-understanding.

"We will want bigger ships," he mused. "They must mount guns and be heavy enough to take the recoil. This is only a sample; we must design, experiment, build them! Can it be done? ... It *must* be done!" he concluded and turned to the inventor.

"We don't know much about those devils of the stars, and they may have means of attack beyond anything we can conceive, but there is just one way to learn: go up there and find out, and take a licking if we have to. Now, how about taking me up a mile or so in the air?"

THE other smiled in self-deprecation. "I like a good fighter," he said; "I was never one myself. If I had been I would have accomplished more. Yes, you shall go up a mile or so in the air—and a thousand miles beyond." He turned to close the door and seal it fast.

Beside the instrument board he seated himself, and at his touch the generator of the ship came startlingly to life. It grumbled softly at first, then the hoarse sound swelled to a thunderous roar, while the metal grating surged up irresistibly beneath the captain's feet. His weight was intolerable. He sank helplessly to the floor....

Blake was white and shaken when he alighted from the ship an hour later, but his eyes were ablaze with excitement. He stopped to seize the tall man by the shoulders.

"I am only a poor devil of a flying man," he said, "but I am speaking for the whole world right now. You have saved us; you've furnished the means. It is up to us now. You've given us the right to hope that humanity can save itself, if humanity will do it. That's my next job—to convince them. We have less than a year and a half...."

THERE was one precious week wasted while Captain Blake chafed and waited for a conference to be arranged at Washington. A spirit of hopelessness had swept over the world—hopelessness and a mental sloth that killed every hope with the unanswerable argument: "What is the use? It is the end." But a meeting was arranged at Colonel Boynton's insistence, though his superiors scoffed at what he dared suggest.

Blake appeared before the meeting, and he told them what he knew—told it to the last detail, while he saw the looks of amusement or commiseration that passed from man to man.

There were scientists there who asked him coldly a question or two and shrugged a supercilious shoulder; ranking officers of both army and navy who openly excoriated Colonel Boynton for bringing them to hear the wild tale of a half-demented man. It was this that drove Blake to a cold frenzy.

The weeks of hopeless despair had worn his nerves to the breaking point, and now, with so much to be done, and so little time in which to do it, all requirements of official etiquette were swept aside as he leaped to his feet to face the unbelieving men.

"Damn it!" he shouted, "will you sit here now and quibble over what you think in your wisdom is possible or not. Get outside those doors—there's an open park beyond—and I'll knock your technicalities all to hell!"

The door slammed behind him before the words could be spoken to place him under arrest, and he tore across a velvet lawn to leap into a taxi.

There was a rising storm of indignant protest within the room that he had left. There were admirals, purple of face, who made heated remarks about the lack of discipline in the army, and generals who turned accusingly where the big figure of Colonel Boynton was still seated.

It was the Secretary of War who stilled the tumult and claimed the privilege of administering the rebuke which was so plainly needed. "Colonel Boynton," he said, and there was no effort to soften the cutting edge of sarcasm in his voice, "it was at your request and suggestion that this outrageous meeting was held. Have you any more requests or suggestions?"

The colonel rose slowly to his feet.

"Yes, Mr. Secretary," he said coldly, "I have. I know Captain Blake. He seldom makes promises; when he does he makes good. My suggestion is that you do what the gentleman said—step outside and see your technicalities knocked to hell." He moved unhurriedly toward the door.

IT was a half-hour's wait, and one or two of the more openly skeptical had left when the first roar came faintly from above. Colonel Boynton led the others to the open ground before the building. "I have always found Blake a man of his word," he said quietly, and pointed upward where a tiny speck was falling from a cloud-flecked sky.

Captain Blake had had little training in the operation of the ship, but he had flown it across the land and had concealed it where fellow officers were sworn to secrecy. And he felt that he knew how to handle the controls.

But the drop from those terrible heights was a fearful thing, and it ended only a hundred feet above the heads of the cowering, shouting humans who crouched under the thunderous blast, where a great shell checked its vertical flight and rebounded to the skies.

Again and again the gleaming cylinder drove at them like a projectile from the mortars of the gods, and it roared and thundered through the air or turned to vanish with incredible speed straight up into the heights, to return and fall again ... until finally it hung motionless a foot above the grass from which the uniformed figures had fled. Only Colonel Boynton was there to greet the flyer as he laid his strange craft gently down.

"Nice little show, Captain," he said, while his broad face broke into the widest of grins. "A damn nice little show! But take that look off of your face. They'll listen to you now; they'll eat right out of your hand."

CHAPTER XV

IF Lieutenant McGuire could have erased from his mind the thought of the threat that hung over the earth he would have found nothing but intensest pleasure in the experiences that were his.

But night after night they had heard the reverberating echoes of the giant gun speeding its messenger of death toward the earth, and he saw as plainly as if he were there the terrible destruction that must come where the missiles struck. Gas, of course; that seemed the chief and only weapon of these monsters, and Djorn, the elected leader of the Venus folk, confirmed him in this surmise.

"We had many gases," he told McGuire, "but we used them for good ends. You people of Earth—or these invaders, if they conquer Earth—must some day engage in a war more terrible than wars between men. The insects are your greatest foe. With a developing civilization goes the multiplication of insect and bacterial life. We used the gases for that war, and we made this world a heaven." He sighed regretfully for his lost world.

"These red ones found them, and our factories for making them. But they have no gift for working out or mastering the other means we had for our defense—the electronic projectors, the creation of tremendous magnetic fields: you saw one when we destroyed the attacking ships. Our scientists had gone far—"

"I wish to Heaven you had some of them to use now," said the lieutenant savagely, and the girl, Althora, standing near, smiled in sympathy for the flyer's distress. But her brother, Djorn, only murmured: "The lust to kill: that is something to be overcome."

The fatalistic resignation of these folk was disturbing to a man of action like McGuire. His eyes narrowed, and his lips were set for an abrupt retort when Althora intervened.

"Come," she said, and took the flyer's hand. "It is time for food."

SHE took him to the living quarters occupied by her brother and herself, where opal walls and jewelled inlays were made lovely by the soft light that flooded the rooms.

"Just one tablet," she said, and brought him a thin white disc, "then plenty of water. You must take this compressed food often and in small quantities till your system is accustomed."

"You make this?" he asked.

"But certainly. Our chemists are learned men. We should lack for food, otherwise, here in our underground home."

He let the tablet dissolve in his mouth. Althora leaned forward to touch his hand gently.

"I am sorry," she said, "that you and Djorn fail to understand one another. He is good—so good! But you—you, too, are good, and you fear for the safety of your own people."

"They will be killed to the last woman and child," he replied, "or they will be captured, which will be worse."

"I understand," she told him, and pressed his hand; "and if I can help, Lieutenant Mack Guire, I shall be so glad."

He smiled at her stilted pronunciation of his name. He had had the girl for an almost constant companion since his arrival; the sexes, he found, were on a level of mutual freedom, and the girl's companionship was offered and her friendship expressed as openly as might have been that of a youth. Of Sykes he saw little; Professor Sykes was deep in astronomical discussions with the scientists of this world.

But she was charming, this girl of a strange race so like his own. A skin from the velvet heart of a rose and eyes that looked deep into his and into his mind when he permitted; eyes, too, that could crinkle to ready laughter or grow misty when she sang those weird melodies of such thrilling sweetness.

Only for the remembrance of Earth and the horrible feeling of impotent fury, Lieutenant McGuire would have found much to occupy his thoughts in this loveliest of companions.

HE laughed now at the sounding of his name, and the girl laughed with him.

"But it *is* your name, is it not?" she asked.

"Lieutenant Thomas McGuire," he repeated, "and those who like me call me 'Mac.'"

"Mac," she repeated. "But that is so short and hard sounding. And what do those who love you say?"

The flyer grinned cheerfully. "There aren't many who could qualify in that respect, but if there were they would call me Tommy."

"That is better," said Althora with engaging directness; "that is much better—Tommy." Then she sprang to her feet and hurried him out where some further wonders must be seen and exclaimed over without delay. But Lieutenant McGuire saw the pink flush that crept into her face, and his own heart responded to the telltale betrayal of her feeling for him. For never in his young and eventful life had the man found anyone who seemed so entirely one with himself as did this lovely girl from a distant star.

He followed where she went dancing on her way, but not for long could his mind be led away from the menace he could not forget. And on this day, as on many days to come, he struggled and racked his brain to find some way in which he could thwart the enemy and avert or delay their stroke.

IT was another day, and they were some months on their long journey away from the earth when an inspiration came. Althora had offered to help, and he knew well how gladly she would aid him; the feeling between them had flowered into open, if unspoken love. Not that he would subject her to any danger—he himself would take all of that when it came—but meanwhile—

"Althora," he asked her, "can you project your mind into that of one of the reds?"

"I could, easily," she replied, "but it would not be pleasant. Their minds are horrible; they reek of evil things." She shuddered at the thought, but the man persisted.

"But if you could help, would you be willing? I can do so little; I can never stop them; but I may save my people from some suffering at least. Here is my idea:

"Djorn tells me that I had it figured right: they plan an invasion of the earth when next the two planets approach. He has told me of their armies and their fleets of ships that will set off into space. I can't prevent it; I am helpless! But if I knew what their leader was thinking—"

"Torg!" she exclaimed. "You want to know the mind of that beast of beasts!"

"Yes," said the man. "It might be of value. Particularly if I could know something of their great gun—where it is and what it is—well, I might do something about that."

The girl averted her eyes from the savage determination on his face. "No—no!" she exclaimed; "I could not. Not Torg!"

McGuire's own face fell at the realization of the enormity of this favor he had demanded. "That's all right," he said and held her soft hand in his; "just forget it. I shouldn't have asked."

But she whispered as she turned to walk away: "I must think, I must think. You ask much of me, Tommy; but oh, Tommy, I would do much for you!" She was sobbing softly as she ran swiftly away.

And the man in khaki—this flyer of a distant air-service—strode blindly off to rage and fume at his helplessness and his inability to strike one blow at those beings who lived in that world above.

THERE were countless rooms and passages where the work of the world below went on. There were men and women whose artistic ability found outlet in carvings and sculpture, chemists and others whose work was the making of foods and endless experimentation, some thousand of men and women in the strength of their endless youth, who worked for the love of the doing and lived contentedly and happily while they waited for the day of their liberation. But of fighters there were none, and for this Lieutenant McGuire grieved wholeheartedly.

He was striding swiftly along where a corridor ended in blackness ahead. There was a gleaming machine on the floor beside him when a hand clutched at his arm and a warning voice exclaimed: "No further, Lieutenant McGuire; you must not go!"

"Why?" questioned the lieutenant. "I've got to walk—do something to keep from this damnable futile thinking."

"But not there," said the other; "it is a place of death. Ten paces more and you would have vanished in a flicker of flame. The projector"—he touched the mechanism beside them—"is always on. Our caves extend in an endless succession; they join with the labyrinth where the red ones used to live. They could attack us but for this. Nothing can live in its invisible ray; they are placed at all such entrances."

"Yet Djorn," McGuire told himself slowly, "said they had no weapons. He knows nothing of war. But, great heavens! what wouldn't I give for a regiment of scrappers—good husky boys with their faces tanned and a spark in their eyes and their gas masks on their chests. With a regiment, and equipment like this—"

And again he realized the futility of armament with none to serve and direct it.

IT was a month or more before Althora consented to the tests. Djorn advised against it and made his protest emphatic, but here, as in all things, Althora was a free agent. It was her right to do as she saw fit, and there was none to prevent in this small world where individual liberty was unquestioned.

And it was still longer before she could get anything of importance. The experiments were racking to her nerves, and McGuire, seeing the terrible strain upon her, begged her to stop. But Althora had gained the vision that was always before her loved one's eyes—a world of death and disaster—and he, here where the bolt would be launched, and powerless to prevent. She could not be dissuaded now.

It was a proud day for Althora when she sent for McGuire, and he found her lying at rest, eyes closed in her young face that was lined and tortured with the mental horror she was contacting. She silenced his protests with a word.

"The gun," she whispered; "they are talking about the gun ... and the bombardment ... planning...."

More silent concentration. Then:

"The island of Bergo," she said, "—remember that! The gun is there ... a great bore in the earth ... solid rock ... but the casing of titanite must be reinforced ... and bands shrunk about the muzzle that projects ... heavy bands ... it shows signs of distortion—the heat!..."

She was listening to the thoughts, and selecting those that bore upon gun.

"... Only fifty days ... the bombardment must begin ... Tahnor has provided a hundred shells; two thousand tals of the green gas-powder in each one ... the explosive charges ready ... yes—yes!..."

"Oh!" she exclaimed and opened her troubled eyes. "The beast is so complacent, so sure! And the bombardment will begin in fifty days! Will it really cause them anguish on your Earth, Tommy?"

"Just plain hell; that's all!"

McGuire's voice was low; his mind was reaching out to find and reject one plan after another. The gun!... He must disable it; he could do that much at least. For himself—well, what of it?—he would die, of course.

The guard he had been taught to place about his own thoughts must have relaxed, for Althora cried out in distress.

"No—no!" she protested; "you shall not! I have tried to help you, Tommy dear—say that I have helped you!—but, oh, my beloved, do not go. Do not risk your life to silence this one weapon. They would still have their ships. Remember what Djorn has told of their mighty fleets, their thousands of fighting men. You cannot stop them; you can hardly hinder them. And you would throw away your life! Oh, please do not go!"

McGuire was seated beside her. His face was hidden in one hand while the other was held tight between the white palms of Althora's tense hands. He said nothing, and he shielded his eyes and locked his mind against her thought force.

"Tommy," said Althora, and now her voice was all love and softness, "Tommy, my dear one! You will not go, for what can you do? And if you stay—oh, my dear!—you can have what you will—the secret of life shall be yours—to live forever in perpetual youth. You may have that. And me, Tommy.... Would you throw your life away in a hopeless attempt, when life might hold so much? Am I offering so little, Tommy?"

And still the silence and the hand that kept the eyes from meeting hers; then a long-drawn breath and a slim figure in khaki that stood unconsciously erect to look, not at the girl, but out beyond the solid walls, through millions of miles of space, to the helpless speck called Earth.

"You offer me heaven, my dear," he spoke softly. "But sometimes"—and his lips twisted into a ghost of a smile—"sometimes, to earn our heaven, we have to fight like hell. And, if we fail to make the fight, what heaven worth having is left?

"And the people," he said softly; "the homes in the cities and towns and villages. My dear, that's part of loving a soldier: you can never own him altogether; his allegiance is divided. And if I failed my own folk what right would I have to you?"

HE dared to look at the girl who lay before him. That other vision was gone but he had seen a clear course charted, and now, with his mind at rest, he could smile happily at the girl who was looking up at him through her tears.

She rose slowly to her feet and stood before him to lay firm hands upon his shoulders. She was almost as tall as he, and her eyes, that had shaken off their tears but for a dewy fringe, looked deep and straight into his.

"We have thought," she said slowly, "we people of this world, that we were superior to you and yours; we have accepted you as someone a shade below our plane of advancement. Yes, we have dared to believe that. But I know better. We have gone far, Tommy, we people of this star; we have lived long. Yet I am wondering if we have lost some virtues that are the heritage of a sterner race.

"But I am learning, Tommy; I am so thankful that I can learn and that I have had you to teach me. We will go together, you and I. We will fight our fight, and, the Great One willing, we will earn our heaven or find it elsewhere—together."

She leaned forward to kiss the tall man squarely upon the lips with her own soft rose-petal lips that clung and clung ... and the reply of Lieutenant McGuire, while it was entirely wordless, seemed eminently satisfactory.

ALTHORA, the beautiful daughter of Venus, had the charm and allure of her planet's fabled namesake. But she thought like a man and she planned like a man. And there was no dissuading her from her course. She was to fight beside McGuire—that was her intention—and beyond that there was no value in argument. McGuire was forced to accept the insistent aid, and he needed help.

Sykes dropped his delving into astronomical lore and answered to the call, but there was no other assistance. Only the three, McGuire, Althora and Sykes. There were some who would agree to pilot the submarine that was being outfitted, but they would have no part in the venture beyond transporting the participants.

More than once McGuire paused to curse silently at the complaisance of this people. What could he not do if they would help. Ten companies of trained men, armed with their deadly electronic projectors that disintegrated any living thing they reached—and he would clutch at his tousled hair and realize that they were only three, and go grimly back to work.

"I don't know what we can do till we get there," he told Sykes. "Here we are, and there is the gun: that is all we know, except that the thing must be tremendous and our only hope is that there is some firing mechanism that we can destroy. The gun itself is a great drilling in the solid rock, lined with one of their steel alloys, and with a big barrel extending up into the air: Althora has learned that.

"They went deep into the rock and set the firing chamber there; it's heavy enough to stand the stress. They use a gas-powder, as Althora calls it, for the charge, and the same stuff but deadlier is in the shell. But they must have underground workings for loading and firing. Is there a chance for us to get in there, I wonder! There's the big barrel that projects. We might ... but no!—that's too big for us to tackle, I'm afraid."

"How about that electronic projector on the submarine?" Sykes suggested. "Remember how it melted out the heart of that big ship? We could do a lot with that."

"Not a chance! Djorn and the others have strictly forbidden the men to turn it on the enemy since they have given no offense.

"No offense!" he repeated, and added a few explosive remarks.

"No, it looks like a case of get there and do what dirty work we can to their mechanism before they pot us—and that's that!"

BUT Sykes was directing his thoughts along another path.

"I wonder ..." he mused; "it might be done: they have laboratories."

"What are you talking about? For the love of heaven, man, if you've got an idea, let's have it. I'm desperate."

"Nitrators!" said the scientist. "I have been getting on pretty good terms with the scientific crowd here, and I've seen some mighty pretty manufacturing laboratories. And they have equipment that was never meant for the manufacture of nitro-explosives, but, with a few modifications—yes, I think it could be done."

"You mean nitro-glycerine? TNT?"

"Something like that. Depends upon what materials we can get to start with."

The lieutenant was pounding his companion upon the back and shouting his joy at this faintest echo of encouragement.

"We'll plant it alongside the gun—No, we'll get into their working underground. We'll blow their equipment into scrap-iron, and perhaps we can even damage the gun itself!" He was almost beside himself with excitement at thought of a weapon being placed in his straining helpless hands.

IT was the earth-shaking thunder of the big gun that hastened their final preparations and made McGuire tremble with suppressed excitement where he helped Sykes to draw off a syrupy liquid into heavy crystal flasks.

There were many of these, and the two men would allow no others to touch them, but stored them themselves and nested each one in a soft bed within the submarine. Then one last repetition of their half-formed plans to Djorn and his followers and a rush toward the wharf where the submarine was waiting.

Althora was waiting, too, and McGuire wasted minutes in a petition that he knew was futile.

"Wait here, Althora," he begged. "I will come back; this is no venture for you to undertake. I can take my chances with them, but you—! It is no place for you," he concluded lamely.

"There is no other place for me," she said; "only where you are." And she led the way while the others followed into the lighted control room of the big under-water craft.

McGuire's eyes were misty with a blurring of tears that were partly from excitement, but more from a feeling of helpless remonstrance that was mingled with pure pride. And his lips were set in a straight line.

The magnetic pull that held them to their anchorage was reversed; the ship beneath them was slipping smoothly beneath the surface and out to sea, guided through its tortuous windings of water-worn caves and rocky chambers under the sea by the invisible electric cords that drew it where they would.

And ahead on some mysterious island was a gun, a thing of size and power beyond anything of Earth. He was going to spike that gun if it was the last act of his life; and Althora was going with him. He drew her slim body to him, while his eyes stared blindly, hopefully, toward what the future held.

CHAPTER XVI

THROUGHOUT the night they drove hour after hour at terrific speed. The ship was running submerged, for McGuire was taking no slightest chance of their being observed from the air. He and the others slept at times, for the crew that handled the craft very evidently knew the exact course, and there were mechanical devices that insured their safety. A ray was projected continuously ahead of them; it would reflect back and give on an indicator instant warning of any derelict or obstruction. Another row of quivering needles gave by the same method the soundings from far ahead.

But the uncertainty of what their tomorrow might hold and the worry and dread lest he find himself unable to damage the big gun made real rest impossible for McGuire.

But he was happy and buoyant with hope when, at last, the green light from the ports showed that the sun was shining up above, and the slackening drive of the submarine's powerful motors told that their objective was in sight.

They lay quietly at last while a periscope of super-sensitiveness was thrust cautiously above the water. It brought in a panoramic view of the shoreline ahead, amplified it and projected the picture in clear-cut detail upon a screen. If Lieutenant McGuire had stood on the wet deck above and looked directly at the island the sight could have been no clearer. The colors of torn and blasted tree-growths showed in all their pale shades, and there was stereoscopic depth to the picture that gave no misleading illusions as to distance.

The shore was there with the white spray of breakers on a rocky shoal, and a beach beyond. And beyond that, in hard outline against a golden sky, was a gigantic tube that stood vertically in air to reach beyond the upper limits of the periscope's vision.

MCGUIRE tingled at the sight. To be within reach of this weapon that had sent those blasting, devastating missiles upon the earth! He paced back and forth in the small room to stop and stare again, and resume his pacing that helped to while away the hours they must wait. For there were man-shapes swarming over the land, and the dull, blood-red of their loose uniforms marked them as members of the fighting force spawned by this prolific breed.

"Not a chance until they're out of the picture," said the impatient man; "they would snow us under. It's just as I thought: we must wait until the gun is ready to fire; then they will beat it. They won't want to be around when that big boy cuts loose."

"And then?" asked Althora.

"Then Sykes and I will take our collection of gallon flasks ashore, and I sure hope we don't stumble." He grinned cheerfully at the girl.

"That reinforced concrete dome seems to be where they get down into the ground; it is close to the base of the gun. We will go there—blow it open if we have to—but manage in some way to get down below. Then a time-fuse on the charge, and the boat will take me off, and we will leave as fast as these motors can drive us."

He omitted to mention any possible danger to Sykes and himself in the handling of their own explosive, and he added casually, "You will stay here and see that there is no slip-up on the getaway."

He had to translate the last remark into language the girl could understand. But Althora shook her head.

"You do try so hard to get rid of me, Tommy," the laughed, "but it is no use. I am going with you—do not argue—and I will help you with the attack. Three will work faster than two—and I am going."

McGuire was silent, then nodded his assent. He was learning, this Earthman, what individual freedom really meant.

ONLY the western sky showed golden masses on the shining screen when McGuire spoke softly to the captain:

"Your men will put us ashore; you may ask them to stand by now." And to Professor Sykes, "Better get that 'soup' of yours ready to load."

The red-clad figures were growing dim on the screen, and the blotches of colors that showed where they were grouped were few. Some there were who left such groups to flee precipitately toward a waiting airship.

This was something the lieutenant had not foreseen. He had expected that the force that served the gun would have some shock-proof shelter; he had not anticipated a fighting ship to take them away.

"That's good," he exulted; "that is a lucky break. If they just get out of sight we will have the place to ourselves."

There were no red patches on the screen now, and the picture thrown before them showed the big ship, its markings of red and white distinct even in the shadow-light of late afternoon, rising slowly into the air. It gathered speed marvelously and vanished to a speck beyond the land.

"We're getting the breaks," said McGuire crisply. "All right—let's go!"

The submarine rose smoothly, and the sealed doors in the superstructure were opened while yet there was water to come trickling in. Men came with a roll of cloth that spread open to the shape of a small boat, while a metal frame expanded within it to hold it taut.

McGuire gasped with dismay as a seaman launched it and leaped heavily into the frail shell to attach a motor to one end.

"Metal!" the captain reassured him; "woven metal, and water-tight! You could not pierce it with anything less than a projector."

SYKES was ready with one of the crystal flasks as the boat was brought alongside, and McGuire followed with another. They took ten of the harmless-looking containers, and both men held their breaths as the boat grounded roughly on the boulder-strewn shore.

They lifted them out and bedded them in the sand, then returned to the submarine. This time Althora, too, stepped into the boat. They loaded in the balance of the containers; the motor purred. Another landing, and they stood at last on the island, where a mammoth tube towered into the sky and the means for its destruction was at their feet.

But there was little time; already the light was dimming, and the time for the firing of the big weapon was drawing near. The men worked like mad to carry the flasks to the base of the gun, where a dome of concrete marked the entrance to the rooms below.

Each man held a flask of the deadly fluid when Althora led the way where stairs went deep down into the earth under the domed roof. This part of the work had been foreseen, and the girl held a slender cylinder that threw a beam of light, intensely bright.

They found a surprising simplicity in the arrangements underground. Two rooms only had been carved from the solid rock, and one of these ended in a wall of gray metal that could be only the great base of the gun. But nowhere was a complication of mechanism that might be damaged or destroyed, nor any wiring or firing device.

A round door showed sharp edges in the gray metal, but only the strength of many men could have removed its huge bolts, and these two knew there must be other doors to seal in the mighty charge.

"Not a wire!" the scientist exclaimed. "How do they fire it?" The answer came to him with the question.

"Radio, of course; and the receiving set is in the charge itself; the barrel of the gun is its own antenna. They must fire it from a distance—back on the island where we were, perhaps. It would need to be accurately timed."

"Come on!" shouted McGuire, and raised the flask of explosive to his shoulder.

EACH one knew the need for haste; each waited every moment for the terrible blast of gun-fire that would jar their bodies to a lifeless pulp or, by detonating their own explosive, destroy them utterly. But they carried the flasks again to the top, and the three of them worked breathlessly to place their whole supply where McGuire directed.

The massive barrel of the gun was beside them; it was held in tremendous castings of metal that bolted to anchorage in the ground. One great brace had an overhanging flange; the explosive was placed beneath it.

Professor Sykes had come prepared. He attached a detonator to one of the flasks, and while the other two were placing the explosive in position he fastened two wires to the apparatus with steady but hurrying fingers; then at full speed he ran with the spool from which the wires unwound.

McGuire and Althora were behind him, running for the questionable safety of the sand-hills. Sykes stopped in the shelter of a tiny valley where winds had heaped the sand.

"Down!" he shouted. "Get down—behind that sand dune, there!"

He dropped beside them, the bared ends of the wires in his hands. There was a battery, too, a case no larger than his hands. Professor Sykes, it appeared, had gained some few concessions from his friends, who had learned to respect him in the field of science.

One breathless moment he waited; then—

"Now!" he whispered, and touched the battery's terminals with the bare wires.

TO McGuire it seemed, in that instant of shattering chaos, that the great gun itself must have fired. He had known the jar of heavy artillery at close range; he had had experience with explosives. He had even been near when a government arsenal had thrown the countryside into a hell of jarring, ear-splitting pandemonium. But the concussion that shook the earth under him now was like nothing he had known.

The hill of sand that sheltered them vanished to sweep in a sheet above their heads. And the air struck down with terrific weight, then left them in an airless void that seemed to make their bodies swell and explode. It rushed back in a whirling gale to sweep showers of sand and pebbles over the helpless forms of the three who lay battered and stunned.

An instant that was like an age; then the scientist pointed with a weak and trembling hand where a towering spire of metallic gray leaned slowly in the air. So slowly it moved, to the eyes of the watchers—a great arc of gathering force and speed that shattered the ground where it struck.

"The gun!" was all that the still-dazed lieutenant could say. "The—the gun!" And he fell to shivering uncontrollably, while tears of pure happiness streamed down his face.

The mammoth siege gun—the only weapon for bombardment of the helpless Earth—was a mass of useless metal, a futile thing that lay twisted and battered on the sands of the sea.

THE submarine now showed at a distance; it had withdrawn, by prearrangement, to the shelter of the deeper water. McGuire looked carefully at the watch on his wrist, and listened to make certain that the explosion had not stopped it. Sykes had told him the length of the Venusian day—twenty hours and nineteen minutes of Earth time, and he had made his calculations from the day of the Venusians. And, morning and night, McGuire had set his watch back and had learned to make a rough approximation of the time of that world.

The watch now said five-thirteen, and the sun was almost gone; a line of gold in the western sky; and McGuire knew that it was a matter only of minutes till the blast of the big gun would rock the island. One heavy section of the great barrel was resting upon the shattered base, and McGuire realized that this blocking of the monster's throat must mean it would tear itself and the island around it to fragments when it fired. He ran toward the beach and waved his arms wildly in air to urge on the speeding craft that showed dim and vague across the heaving sea.

It drove swiftly toward them and stopped for the launching of the little boat. There was a delay, and McGuire stood quivering with impatience where the others, too, watched the huddle of figures on the submarine's deck.

It was Althora who first sensed their danger. Her voice was shrill with terror as she seized McGuire's arm and pointed landward.

"Tommy—Tommy!" she said. "They are coming! I saw them!"

A SWARMING of red figures over the nearby dunes gave quick confirmation of her words. McGuire looked about him for a weapon—anything to add efficiency to his bare hands—and the swarm was upon them as he looked.

He leaped quickly between Althora and the nearest figures that stretched out grasping hands, and a red face went white under the smashing impact of the flyer's fist.

They poured over the sand-hills now——scores of leaping man-shapes—and McGuire knew in an instant of self-accusation that there had been a shelter after all, where a portion of the enemy force had stayed. The explosion had brought them, and now—

He struck in a raging frenzy at the grotesque things that came racing upon them. He knew Sykes was fighting too. He tore wildly at the lean arms that bound him and kept him from those a step or two away who were throwing the figure of a girl across the shoulders of one of their men, while her eyes turned hopelessly toward McGuire.

They threw the two men upon the sand and crowded to kneel on the prostrate bodies and strike and tear with their long hands, then tied them at ankles and wrists with metal cords, and raised them helpless and bound in the air.

One of the red creatures pointed a long arm toward the demolished gun and shrieked something in a terror-filled tone. The others, at the sound, raced off through the sand, while those with the burden of the three captives followed as best they could.

"The gun!" said Professor Sykes in a thick voice: the words were jolted out of him as the two who carried him staggered and ran. "They know—that it—hasn't—gone off—"

THE straggling troop that strung out across the dim-lit dunes was approaching another domed shelter of heavy concrete. They crowded inside, and the bodies of the three were thrown roughly to the floor, while the red creatures made desperate haste to close the heavy door. Then down they went into the deeper safety of a subterranean room, where the massive walls about them quivered to a nerve-deadening jar. It shook those standing to the floor, and the silence that followed was changed to a bedlam by the inhuman shrieking of the creatures who were gloating over their safety and the capture they had achieved. They leaped and capered in a maniacal outburst and ceased only at the shrill order of one who was in command.

At his direction the three were carried out of doors and thrown upon the ground. McGuire turned his head to see the face of Althora. There was blood trickling from a cut on her temple, and her eyes were dazed and blurred, but she managed a trembling smile for the anxious eyes of the man who could only struggle hopelessly against the thin wires that held him.

Althora hurt! Bound with those cutting metal cords! Althora—in such beastly hands! He groaned aloud at the thought.

"You should never have come; I should never have let you. I have got you into this!" He groaned again in an agony of self-reproach, then lay silent and waited for what must come. And the answer to his speculations came from the night above, where the lights of a ship marked the approach of an enemy craft.

THE ships of the red race could travel fast, as McGuire knew, but the air monster whose shining, pointed beak hung above them where they lay helpless in the torturing bonds of fine wire, was to give him a new conception of speed.

It shot to the five thousand-foot level, when the captives were safe aboard, and the dark air shrieked like a tortured animal where the steel shell tore it to tatters. And the radio, in an adjoining room, never ceased in its sputtering, changing song.

The destruction of the Earth-bombarding gun! The capture of the two Earth-men who had dared to fight back! And a captive woman of the dreaded race of true Venusians! There was excitement and news enough for one world. And the discordant singing of the radio was sounding in the ears of the leaders of that world.

They were waiting on the platform in the great hall where Sykes and McGuire had stood, and their basilisk eyes glared unwinkingly down at the three who were thrown at their feet.

The leader of them all, Torg himself, arose from his ornate throne and strode forward for a closer view of the trophies his huntsmen had brought in. A whistled word from him and the wires that had bound Althora's slim ankles were cut, while a red-robed warrior dragged her roughly to her feet to stand trembling and swaying as the blood shot cruelly through her cramped limbs.

Torg's eyes to McGuire were those of a devil feasting on human flesh, as he stared appraisingly and gloatingly at the girl who tried vainly to return the look without flinching. He spoke for a moment in a harsh tone, and the seated councilors echoed his weird notes approvingly.

"What does he say?" McGuire implored, though he knew there could be nothing of good in that abominable voice. "What does he say, Althora?"

THE face that turned slowly to him was drained of the last vestige of color. "I—do not—know," she said in a whisper scarcely audible; "but he thinks—terrible things!"

She seemed speaking of some nightmare vision as she added haltingly, "There is a fleet of many ships, and Torg is in command. He has thousands of men, and he goes forth to conquer your Earth. He goes there to rule." She had to struggle to bring the words to her lips now. "And—he takes me—with—him!"

"No—no!" the flyer protested, and he struggled insanely to free his hands from the wires that cut the deeper into his flesh. The voice of Althora, clear and strong now, brought him back.

"I shall never go, Tommy; never! The gift of eternal life is mine, but it is mine to keep only if I will. But, for you and your friend—" She tried to raise her hands to her trembling lips.

"Yes," said Lieutenant McGuire quietly, "for us—?"

But there were some things the soft lips of Althora refused to say. Again she tried vainly to raise her hands, then turned her white, stricken face that a loved one might not see the tears that were mingling with the blood-stains on her cheeks, nor read in her eyes the horror they beheld.

But she found one crumb of comfort for the two doomed men.

"You will live till the sailing of the ships, Tommy," she choked, "and then—we will go together, Tommy—you and I."

Her head was bowed and her shoulders shaking, but she raised her head proudly erect as she was seized by a guard whose blood-red hands forced her from the room.

And the dry, straining eyes of Lieutenant McGuire, that watched her going, saw the passing to an unknown fate of all he held dear, and the end of his unspoken dreams.

He scarcely felt the grip of the hands that seized him, nor knew when he and Sykes were carried from the room where Torg, the Emperor, held his savage court. The stone walls of the room where they were thrown could not hold his eyes; they looked through and beyond to see only the white and piteous face of a girl whose lips were whispering: "We will go together, Tommy—you and I."

(Concluded in the next issue)

MYSTERIOUS CARLSBAD CAVERN

THE largest cavern ever discovered, at Carlsbad Cavern, N. M., is soon going to be explored.

Carlsbad Cavern is so large that that three sky-scrapers a half-mile apart could be built in the largest of its innumerable "rooms," according to Mr. Nicholson, who was there once before, about a year ago. Only 22 miles of the cavern's apparently limitless tunnels have been explored, revealing such natural beauties that President Coolidge established it as a national monument.

The stalagmites in the cavern tower 100 feet high. The age of the cavern was put at 60,000,000 years by Dr. Willis T. Lee of the National Geographic Society, after his survey three years ago.

The caverns were discovered fifteen years ago by a New Mexican cowboy named Jim White, according to Mr. Nicholson. White was riding across a desert waste one day when he saw what appeared to be smoke from a volcano. After riding three hours in the direction of the smoke he discovered that it was an enormous cloud of bats issuing from the mouth of a gigantic cavern. He decided the cavern deserved exploration, and a few years later he and a Mexican boy were lowered in a barrel over the 750-foot cliff which overhangs the cavern.

The stalagmites of the cavern, according to Mr. Nicholson, are very vibrant and resonant. One can play a "xylophone solo" on them with practice, he said, but it is dangerous, since a certain pitch would crack them.

The temperature of the cavern is 56 degrees Fahrenheit, never varies, day and night, winter and summer. The air is purified every twenty-four hours in some mysterious fashion, though there are no air currents. This is explained by the theory that there exists a great subterranean stream at a lower level, probably 1,200 feet down.

Specimens of stalagmites will be collected and reconstructed for the American Museum of Natural History. The explorers expect to find also flying fish, flying salamanders, rare insects and thousands of bats. A Government representative will go along, and drawings and motion pictures will be made.

www.ingramcontent.com/pod-product-compliance
Ingram Content Group UK Ltd.
Pitfield, Milton Keynes, MK11 3LW, UK
UKHW031837270325
456796UK00003B/369